Praise for

Conscious Whole Being
A Return to Wholeness

"It is a true pleasure and honor to recommend Deborah Hall's fine offering to the world of conscious integration. She has done her homework; she has entered into that fearsome inner world of doubt and confusion to return with an even greater sense of herself. As such, she has become that rare teacher who, through personal experience, can now write this fine primer and reference on the essential approach for this deep inner journey. And fortunately, she names the things we each must be willing to engage, the obstacles we will encounter, and the first clear steps we must take in order for our inner wisdom to emerge and guide us into our own self-awakening, which is the path each soul must ultimately take. In this book, you will also find the groundwork of the new and truer psychotherapy that must emerge to meet the current challenges of deep integration and growth."

> —Rick Gutierrez, BodyMind Integration Instructor,
> Developer of *Integrative Tracking*

"*Conscious Whole Being Integration: A Return to Wholeness* is a much needed holistic and open-hearted look at the process of becoming the most we can be. Deborah's unerring yet gentle critique of the cold and clinically detached approach to human development work revives the individual, balances the student-mentor relationship, and rescues the individual from a mere patient to the driver of a true process of self-knowing. The result is a wise and studied process which returns empathy and balance to the often sterile Allopathic and Pharmaceutical paradigm. I highly recommend this idealistic and yet pragmatic book."

> —Jeffrey Armstrong (Kavindra Rishi), Vedic Teacher
> and Yoga Psychologist

"As someone working in the mental health field, the concepts of self-awareness and enlightenment are just that: concepts. In reading this book, I was awakened to the possibility of an *experiential* inward journey of myself that encompassed the body, mind, and soul. The author drew from her own experiences to educate, inform, and support those interested in taking the dive inward. I feel as if this book was written just for me!"

> —Chris Beckley M.A. in Clinical Psychology

"Deborah Hall has been on the path for a long time. This incredible book is the result. Deborah brings her deep personal work, as well as her professional work with others, to the page. She offers it as a companion and guide to fellow seekers on paths of their own. Like traveling unchartered territory with a good map, *Conscious Whole Being Integration: A Return to Wholeness* will guide its readers through the sometimes murky waters of self-exploration to a place of greater clarity and self-understanding. For those who find this book, this book will help them find themselves."

—Jason Scholder, Teacher of Yoga and Meditation

"I have been on my spiritual path for several decades and have tried various therapies with varying degrees of success, but always come back to my same core issues. After reading Deborah Hall's book, I realized that there is a piece of the therapeutic puzzle that no one else seems to be 'getting' or addressing: bodymind integration. The body itself has a consciousness that needs to be acknowledged and worked with in concert with the emotional and mental aspects of an individual's consciousness. This is cutting-edge work, not easy to do, but absolutely essential for anyone seeking spiritual evolution, true healing, and ultimate health on all levels of their being. Fortunately, this book is an excellent primer on bodymind integration and provides an excellent starting place for such a journey. One last note: If true healing begins when one feels truly seen by even one other being, the biggest gift you may be able to give yourself is to read this book. Deborah Hall opens up the potential for you to be seen by the most important person you are in relationship with: yourself."

—Deborah Bloom, Author of *Jemimah*

"My journey has led me to at least a dozen different therapists, many self-help seminars, meditation retreats, self-help books and spiritual teachers. Most had some merit, but there was always something missing. Finally, that missing piece is being addressed in this book. The author's way of explaining the inner mechanics of how we function is astounding! Deborah's teachings put into perspective what real bodymind integration means. This groundbreaking book naturally bridges the gap between the world of psychology and spirituality and is a must-read for anyone that wants to experience true internal self-awareness. This read can be challenging at times because *reality* is not always what we want to hear, see or experience. I highly recommend this book for those individuals that want to directly experience *deep* healing and awakening. This is a guidebook for your inner exploration that can be referenced for years to come. I can't wait for her next book!"

—RL, Holistic Health Practitioner, Doctor of Oriental Medicine

"The author, wise from her many years of inner work and clinical study, describes her realization that instead of pathologies which need medicating and fixing, these are the opportunities for spiritual growth and deep healing. The author acknowledges the value as well as the limits of psychotherapy practiced today, and that this incomplete paradigm doesn't answer the longing of the soul to find wholeness. She describes in great detail the deeper path of self-discovery through her personal experience. As such, she provides guidelines to grow naturally throughout life into wholeness. This book is a personal story of self-discovery from one who is now sharing the mastery gained with the world, a book worth spending time with to gain one's bearings in the sea of consciousness we call the human experience."

—E.K., Author, Personal Wealth Manager

"Deborah allows us to follow her personal journey of awakening as she travels on the very challenging road of deep healing and integration. She highlights several of the challenges we each face living in a modern society that exclusively relies on mental health labels and prescription drugs as its main healing modality. This incomplete paradigm fails to treat the underlying *source* of the problem. As such, Deborah provides an alternative path. I highly recommend you start this journey with Deborah! This book serves as a valuable guide for the sincere seeker who is ready to embark on their own inner journey of spiritual awaking and deep healing—a path that ultimately leads to the conscious integration of your *whole being*."

—Joel Hagberg, Marketing Professional

"Along this life's journey, I have talked with a half dozen therapists and spent many years reading self-help books, and seeking answers, but still felt that there was/is something missing. After reading Deborah's book, I knew my unique experiences were being 'fixed,' yielding different results, but I was not truly healing. As Deborah points out in her book, my experiences are real for me and they don't need 'fixing.' Instead, what's called for is my love, self-compassion, and a sincere willingness to acknowledge what I *am* experiencing within myself. I felt the pieces of the disconnected puzzle that was my life start to fall into place and form the picture of who I really am. This book was empowering and helpful to me, and I am certain it will be for others. I look forward to learning more about this process. This book is a great gift to me and to all who seek an awakened healing."

—Virginia Utley, Independent Appraiser

"What I feel is most significant to acknowledge about this book is the explanation of and importance it gives to the 'bodymind' and how, by working with our physiology, as well as our psychology, we can achieve emotional and spiritual healing, health and 'whole being integration.' There is a growing awareness of how important it is to understand how all aspects of our being are interconnected and interrelated, and this book further supports and deepens our understanding as Deborah shares what she has learned through her own personal work, as well as observations from her clinical practice. The emphasis on the uniqueness of the individual journey, developing awareness of our feelings, sensations and inner wisdom, the organic and natural unfolding of the process, the importance of avoiding labels and working with the experience, combined with the emphasis on integration—all provide opportunities for deeper and more holistic healing when compared to approaches that focus on managing symptoms or behaviors. Her title, *Conscious Whole Being Integration: A Return to Wholeness,* is an accurate and honest description of the process she presents in this book. I have been a manual therapist working with somatoemotional processes for many years, and I am grateful that Deborah has shared her insights and knowledge regarding a process that works with the body and the mind in such an integrative way."

—Sheryl McGavin, OTL, CST, Therapist, Teacher

CONSCIOUS WHOLE BEING INTEGRATION

A Return to Wholeness

DEBORAH HALL

The information and advice contained in this book are based upon the research and the personal and professional experiences of the author. They are not intended as a substitute for consulting with a health care professional. The author is not responsible for any adverse effects or consequences resulting from the use of any of the suggestions, preparations, or procedures discussed in this book. All matters pertaining to your physical health should be supervised by a health care professional.

ISBNs: Softcover: 978-0-9978282-0-7
        Hardcover: 978-0-9978282-1-4
        E-book: 978-0-9978282-2-1

Cover and interior design: Gary A. Rosenberg

Printed in the United States of America.

This book is lovingly dedicated to the teachers and
individuals who uniquely supported me through
the many years of my deep inner exploration.

Contents

Acknowledgments

I feel enormously grateful for all the support I have received during the process of writing this book. I would like to thank Mark Henry Bloom for his proficient editing skills and also for his dedication to this project, as well as his encouragement and friendship.

I would also like to acknowledge the teachers who have supported and/or inspired me at various times during my awakening and healing process. I extend my deepest gratitude toward Rick Gutierrez, Michael Mamas, and Adyashanti.

I would like to thank my mother and father for the unique way in which they supported me; it allowed me to live the dharma. Thank you to my four legged children—Alex, Tyler, Shaela, and Sofia—for your friendship and affection.

Lastly, I must thank my husband Daniel Lewis. It's rare to find a partner who supports you exactly as you are, and I have had the good fortune of having a partner who supported the unique unfolding of my inner journey . . . even when it was not conventional, pretty, or easy.

Introduction

I've spent most of my life within the big questions of life and existence. I wanted to understand the deeper mechanics of nature and consciously experience a deep and profound connection to everything.

This desire, this urge, led me to study different spiritual traditions, while simultaneously immersing myself in the field of psychology, bodymind integration, and energy healing. During this exploration, I attained a Masters degree in Clinical Psychology and opened my own private practice.

As a free thinker, it's natural for me to question everything and feel or search inwardly for my own answers. Over the years, I collected many pieces of the puzzle, yet they didn't fit together seamlessly. For all my searching, I couldn't find a natural place of integration deep within myself. Feeling frustrated, I decided to take time off from my private practice to piece together this mystery. What I thought would be a short process of several months ended up lasting nearly two decades, and in many ways, continues today and perhaps for the rest of my life.

As I took a deep dive inward and engaged my full experience on all levels of being, exactly as it was, my perception of myself—and thereby my experience of life and existence—slowly and subtly shifted. What I learned was that *deep healing brings about spiritual awakening, and spiritual awakening brings about deep healing.* You cannot have one without the other.

Once I saw everything from this universal, but new-to-me perspective, I could not go back to the limited way in which I had once functioned. Nor could I practice psychotherapy from the limited perspective I was originally taught. My eyes and ears now opened, I was shocked by the discoveries I made: I could see and feel the many interrelationships that were active within me. I could also feel and track how a distortion on one level affected all other levels. Therefore, in order for deep healing to take place and for my soul to learn and develop, I needed to consciously feel and engage all levels of my being—mental, emotional, physical and spiritual.

The discoveries I made compose the premise of this book. My hope for you is that this book might serve as a guide for your own dive inward. This book can help you become both your own teacher and your own student as you awaken from the spell of the conditioned mind and consciously live the incarnate experience of your spiritual journey.

All the great traditions demand that we experience the teachings personally and individually. For me, this process produced my own teachings, which I call Conscious Whole Being Integration. Each of you will likewise have your own unique experience. I offer this book with humility and sincerity, knowing that it is only part of what you need along your journey and hoping that it serves as a very helpful and important piece.

I wish you profound clarity as you move through the many stages and phases of deep healing, awakening and the conscious embodiment of Spirit.

How to Successfully Use the Information in this Book

Conscious Whole Being Integration is a process of gaining self-awareness. You may initially read this book from an intellectual perspective, but you can't think your way to self-awareness. You may not even realize that you're caught in a loop of thinking, cut off from feeling. Yet that's how most of the world functions . . . without even realizing it.

That's all right. As you read and re-read this book, you'll find sections or phrases that strike you in different ways. As your relationship with yourself changes over time, passages that you glossed over before will suddenly take on deeper meaning. Descriptions that meant nothing to you will become rich and valuable. This is ideal; this process gives you the time to integrate your new awareness into the relative world—and into your entire physiology.

I've purposely reiterated a number of key concepts in each chapter, creating redundancy in this book. While each chapter stands on its own, my initial recommendation would be to read the book from beginning to end. You always have the option to re-read whatever chapters beckon you. It's important to take breaks as you work your way through the material. Move your body when it feels right, and proceed at a pace that's comfortable for you to assimilate the information.

Everyone learns in different ways, and if you use this book appropriately, you'll cultivate a foundation from which to evolve your consciousness.

CHAPTER 1

The Root of Existence

We are currently undergoing a significant evolutionary shift in human consciousness. While signs of this shift have appeared in technology, art, and philosophy, they are most apparent in the fields of medicine, health, and healing. For instance, if we explore the subject of health and healing through the narrow scope of the Western medical model, we see individuals diagnosed and given medication as their sole treatment plan. Sometimes this treatment plan is helpful and even life saving, yet often it creates greater problems through a myriad of side effects.

Therefore, many individuals have become concerned with the dangers of prescribed Western medications, especially the popularly prescribed antidepressants and anti-anxiety drugs. Additionally, more and more of us have become dissatisfied not only with the limited perspective of allopathic medicine, but also of a status quo wherein we live our lives on autopilot, living from the personalities we've developed in order to fit in and be accepted.

Many of us feel called to live more consciously—to feel connected to a deeper, fuller, and more profound understanding of our human existence. The archaic models of attaining true health and healing are being uprooted as a more holistic view of life broadens our perspective.

Western cultures have begun to see what Eastern cultures have long understood: that everything is interconnected. A piecemeal approach to healing, and to human evolution, will no longer suffice. We're looking for what will bring us back into alignment with our own true rhythm, that deep place within us where we hear our own true voice and follow our own inner impulse into direct knowing. We're becoming aware that it's only when we are consciously engaged and organically moving from our own unique, natural flow of life, moment-to-moment, that we live our true potential.

Living a truly holistic existence means that we consciously experience ourselves as seamlessly integrated on all levels of being—the physical, mental, emotional, and spiritual. However, many of us live overextended, overstimulated, and outwardly focused lives that keep us disconnected from this fuller expression of ourselves. When we feel constantly overextended, we lose touch with our physical bodies, leaving us unable to physically feel our experiences. Essentially, we become cut off from feeling from our shoulders down. We've interrupted our healthy flow of thinking and feeling to such an extent that we may not even know what we genuinely want.

This disconnection within the *bodymind* keeps us constantly searching outside ourselves to mitigate what we feel inside. It keeps us in a divided state, cut off from our authentic experience, leaving us with almost no ability to wisely navigate the complex territory of our own thoughts, feelings, and emotions. Additionally, this disconnection from the natural flow of life is reflected in our fragmented and superficial view of health, healing, and spiritual evolution. Our conditioning keeps us stuck in unconscious thought patterns that only allow us to repeat more of the "same old, same old."

Unfortunately, this inner dynamic is an expression of our superficial relationship with the nature of life and existence. It has led us so astray that we're now continually *trying to be spiritual* in an effort to feel better about who and what we think we are. We strive to fix or improve ourselves in the name of wanting to be the best person we can be. No matter how laudable this goal may seem, when we function from this limited perspective, we can only create more "issues" to try to fix.

Yet at the core of our existence, we are spiritual beings with the potential to experience the full spectrum of human life. Therefore, what we experience within ourselves, relative to every aspect of being "human," is information about where we're caught, where we're living from our conditioning. Additionally, each of us functions from a different phase or level of consciousness at any given time, and each phase brings unique experiences, as well as challenges.

As we understand and experientially integrate each deeper perspective, we enter into a deeper conscious relationship with life. We begin to move with, as opposed to resist, our own natural and universal flow. We now become aware that resistance only brings more suffering. In contrast, by developing the ability to live what is truly real and really true within us opens us to our own unique experience and expression of the sublime.

The purpose of this book is to support you as you take a dive inward, deep into the root of your being where you can consciously evolve your relationship with life and existence. These teachings will assist you as you awaken to the conditioning of the mind and its relationship to the physical body, the structures of the personality, and the energetic mappings you carry. As you evolve, you'll begin to connect the dots and consciously experience how you co-create your own experience by continuously collapsing into and identifying with your thoughts, beliefs, ideas, associations, and reactions.

Since all true teachings point you back to yourself, you'll discover *your* inner teacher through this process. In order to be fully awake and consciously embodied, you must autonomously function from within your own direct experience of the teachings.

Lastly, you'll discover the degree to which you've become cut off from your physical experience of feeling. This distorted way of functioning—being cut off from feeling—is epidemic, not just in the West, but throughout the entire world. This book not only describes what it means to feel, but it also supports you as you return to the full spectrum of feeling. Coming back into the sensate world of "feeling" is not just necessary, but crucial to true healing and to your evolution.

So find a comfortable spot to join me as we take this dive inward together. Allow yourself to read this book slowly, observing what the words elicit in you. Take frequent breaks and allow yourself to ponder your experience. Then go back to the material and have another look, allowing the unexpected to be revealed as you move deeper inside. I've purposely kept this a foundational book so you can refer back to it again and again as you move through the different layers of your experience. A grounded foundation is imperative for you to move inwardly safely and successfully.

Are you ready to begin *your* journey?

Respecting Your Reality and Stage of Development

Each of us is unique. Just as no two snowflakes are alike, neither can your experience of yourself, of others, nor of life itself be exactly like mine. My reality at any given moment is different from yours. It has to be. We each have our own lessons to learn. So what is medicine for you may be poison for me. What is medicine for everyone, however, is a reunion with self.

If you pretend to be more awake than your direct experience indicates or if you force yourself to try to have a different experience than you're actually having, you block the natural flow of your own innate intelligence, which is your unique gift to yourself and the world. If you want to come back into alignment with your natural inner rhythm, begin to respect your experience *exactly as it is,* however much you may dislike it. When you do this, it realigns you with your own unique and natural flow of life. By setting this intention, you initiate a powerful reunion with what you've avoided: essentially, a reunion with your own unique snowflake self. It's in this honest and authentic relationship to yourself and your inner terrain where you'll gain clarity about how you currently function—and *that* is where true transformation happens. As you become aware of your *relationship* to your early conditioning, that early conditioning organically changes and evolves. But as you'll discover, this is not an easy task.

Typically, we're afraid to be honest with ourselves about

our current experience because of what we fear we may experience. When we become accustomed to changing our thoughts and experience to what we *think* is a preferred reality, in essence, we create a type of split. In order to reconnect with our current experience exactly as it is, it's important to stop, be still, and listen deeply.

As you gain experience at being able to consciously feel, you'll discover for yourself what's an expression of your True Self and what's the limited and limiting expression of your conditioning. Just when you think you know something about yourself absolutely, you'll discover, as you move deeper, that your "experience" is a deceptive expression of your conditioning.

So how do you come back into the natural flow of life after being disconnected from your current experience for so long? In this holistic work and teachings, you'll learn that it happens by degrees . . . and in a non-linear fashion. You sincerely have to want to be with what's real and true along a vast continuum—even if at this actual moment, you can't. In other words, you need a deep motivation to be honest above all else from the beginning. When you move inside, gradually evolving your consciousness and naturally rewiring your physiology, you'll develop a better ability to remain conscious, moment-to-moment, as you move all the way through your experiences. Some of them may feel uncomfortable, while others may feel quite pleasant. Being with both the light *and* the darkness not only provides a broader picture of your relationship to the whole spectrum of existence, but the process matures you spiritually as well.

Some of us are more prepared than others to experience ourselves this directly. It will take sufficient mastery to consciously be with what scares you most without grasping onto it or pushing it away. However, to re-establish an authentic connection and create the conditions for nature to bring about a self-correction of the distortions you carry, this profound ability is one that you'll want to cultivate.

This book prepares you and your physiology, little by little, layer upon layer, to naturally come back to a *conscious whole being integration*. The deeper you go, the more profound your experience becomes. You can't know in advance what level of your being, nor what layer of your story, you'll find yourself unconsciously caught up in. All is revealed as you consciously awaken, moment-to-moment, within and to your direct experience. You might find yourself stuck at early stages of childhood development, in which case you'll want to physically feel, and wisely and compassionately validate, all aspects of your story so the energy can transform and find its release. Or you might find yourself consciously experiencing when a deeply held belief got put into place . . . except this time, you have the ability to consciously move all the way through the experience, feeling and learning from it instead of going unconscious and re-identifying with it. This book examines both situations, and more.

The point is this: you'll remain engaged with your current phase of development or level of consciousness until you learn what you need to learn. As you learn, your consciousness evolves, bringing you into a fuller and more embodied expression of self-awareness. The more profound the experience, the more imperative it is to find a facilitator/teacher who can consciously work on all levels of being with you. Chapter 10 discusses the goals and benefits of finding and working with such a facilitator/teacher.

The Power—and Limitations—of Psychotherapy

Psychotherapy has demonstrated tremendous value for individuals, couples, and families in our culture. It has helped many return to their lives and be functional members of society. But it has its limitations.

In the past, psychotherapy's traditional approach to helping people has been to simply treat psychological pathology. In other words, what's wrong with the patient? Why isn't he functioning as a healthy individual in society? How can he be treated to overcome or manage his dysfunctions or disease?

This is inherently a limited view, and so psychotherapists have had limited success in supporting individuals as they move through the trials and tribulations of their life experiences. In the pathological paradigm, individuals are diagnosed and then given a treatment plan that's designed to help them overcome their dysfunctions by managing their symptoms. Many times, drugs are prescribed as a way to help them function in a more "normal" way again. Many individuals, however, are prescribed antidepressants or other medications for years without any of the recommended psychotherapy. These individuals *are* able to go back out into the world and function again, so it appears as though it's a win-win situation. Yet these patients are not cured; they are only "managed."

So this approach contains a deep flaw in that it creates a deep division within the person, within the self. When a patient is merely managed through a series of internal or external adaptations (such as prescription drugs or behavioral therapy), his system further contorts, eventually exposing a deeply held distortion or imbalance. It has to, because everything is interconnected. It's only a matter of time before the internal distortion causes him to "act out" again as a way to alleviate his suffering. On the surface, the patient may seem to be functioning just fine in everyday life, yet simultaneously an unconscious time bomb is ticking away. An inner charge is building, leaving the individual with no alternative *other than* to unconsciously discharge. Our unconscious relationship to this ticking time bomb is reflected back to us as an ongoing split held within the *bodymind*. Since it's impossible to integrate what we can't feel, all we can do is manage our symptoms, behaviors, and reactions. Deep, organic healing always happens inside first, from the inside out, not from the outside in.

Yet the pathological paradigm can have some value. Individuals who cannot afford long-term therapy have no choice but to function in their current state. If they have families to support, this paradigm can help them manage their symptoms while functioning out in the world. Also, if they have no genuine interest in doing any type of inner exploration, this paradigm can possibly produce the results they're looking for. In order for psychotherapy to be of any true value, the patient has to want to learn about how he functions. Even at its best, however, this modality extracts a price for accepting its limitations.

Psychotherapists are trained to analyze the ways in which their clients do not function "normally." From that diagnosis, they help their clients overcome, manage, or understand their relationship to their emotional and behavioral problems. Many therapists, however, base their course of action on their own preconceptions of what their clients should look like when healthy. When they themselves function from a limited perspective, this is the lens through which they see their clients. Furthermore, they typically don't include the physical body in their explorations. Functioning from such a limited talk-only perspective, they can unknowingly keep a patient stuck with only a limited set of the tools needed to deeply heal and awaken.

At some point, after going round and round, telling their stories while disconnected from physically feeling, these patients may eventually realize they could explore their psychological issues indefinitely through this limited paradigm. It can only take them so far. This realization is often experienced as a shift of consciousness that provides them with sufficient resources to engage their inner life from a fuller and deeper perspective. Instead, they can use their pathologies as a doorway to the truth of their Being. Instead of overcoming, managing, or fixing their experiences, they wisely open to them.

Deep Healing and Awakening

While there will always be a need for prescribed medication to quickly dampen our emotional and psychological pain, *deep healing* happens organically, degrees at a time. True healing emanates from within; it isn't something given to you from an external source. You can't know what you'll look like when healthy; you can only be with your current experience consciously, *as it is.* True healing isn't a condition in which you *emulate* health, but the kind where health is your *direct physiological experience.* You don't have to force yourself to feel or think a certain way; you just *are.*

So the question arises: how can you create the proper

conditions for deep healing and awakening to take place? First, you have to understand how and where healing and awakening occurs: it happens inside, as you become more adept at being with your experience *as it is in the moment,* without having to change, fix, avoid, or grasp onto anything. Acceptance of your experience means that you're not resisting "what is." You don't have to like it or agree with it, but you have to accept that it is what it is.

However, the acceptance of "what is" certainly is not the end point or the goal. It's a surrender that authentically opens your awareness. This opening is an entryway into the inner landscape of your being. It's here where you can become aware of your conditioning—learning about your current relationship with your thoughts, beliefs, associations, ideas and reactions, as well as how you lose yourself and identify with them. You'll do well to include all levels of being and multiple perspectives into your inner exploration. And you'll need to learn how to track and feel your experience within the physical and energetic levels of your being. Through this inner exploration, you gradually develop a conscious awareness of how you operate—how the inner mechanics of your whole being functions, not only on a day-to-day level, but on deeper levels as well.

As you read this book, you'll come to understand that there isn't a single model for healing and awakening yourself. Nature does the healing, not the models you follow. Specific models can potentially have value at different points of your inner exploration. The key is knowing how and when to use them. When you put yourself in any one box, you are limiting your awareness of how you currently function, as well as the full expression of your true nature.

Psychotherapy's Role . . . and Limits

Regardless of its limitations, psychology has made great strides in understanding human suffering and its relationship to early childhood developmental experiences. We have valuable theories and models to help individuals explore themselves. We have qualified practitioners who truly want to help people understand why they feel, act, and react as they do. Being able to make sense of their behavior—and how it connects to their childhood—can make a huge difference in their lives. For example, psychotherapy can help people ease the frustrations that have built up over many years after a childhood in which their individual experience was never respected or validated.

Psychotherapy has also developed support systems and communities, such as the 12-step approach, to give individuals a place to tell their stories and have others bear witness. These communities promote personal accountability and kinship among individuals who can relate and empathize with each other's story. For many individuals, just having someone acknowledge their inner pain does wonders to help them feel more comfortable within themselves.

Yet as I said earlier, psychotherapy in its current paradigm—even with its tremendous value—can only take you so far in your process of human and spiritual evolution. During my years of private practice as a holistic facilitator and psychotherapist, I encountered many individuals who felt frustrated with the limited paradigm of psychotherapy and psychiatry. Despite many years of psychoanalysis, they felt more disconnected from their authentic selves than ever before.

I've also come across many individuals who've had a long-term relationship with analyzing their lives. They habitually try to figure everything out. They believe if they can figure out why they feel like they do, they can overcome their uncomfortable experience of themselves. But it becomes an endless cycle. Psychological theories and models are merely the tools we use for exploring our current experiences. They are helpful because they can show us how we function from a different perspective. Having a new understanding of how we function, though, is only the beginning of the deep healing and integrative process. We must include the deeper layers and levels of our being in the mix.

If you feel like you're going round and round, looping within the confines of your mental/emotional exploration while hoping and striving for a different experience of yourself, then this could be a clue that you're coming up against the limited perspective of psychotherapy's current paradigm. You may be ready to approach your inner life from a broader perspective. This can be a daunting task, especially if you've had years of prescribed psychotherapeutic treatment—be it cognitive and/or behavioral exercises, drugs, rehabs with the 12-step approach, or years of analysis. You may find it difficult to walk away from a modality that you've come to believe will change you. It can feel terrifying. You've read all the right books, and you understand intellectually what it takes for you to appear healthy—or at least what your therapist's or society's notion of what being healthy should look like. Yet are you truly healthy when all you can do is emulate someone else's limited version of health? This cycle can perpetuate itself until you become too sick, too exhausted, or both to keep up the charade. You must experience a deep letting go or surrender before you can begin to acknowledge to yourself what's truly real and true.

Once you have the capacity to quiet yourself and feel inward, you'll find another layer of thoughts and emotions waiting for you, a layer in which your problems can't be medicated away or hidden beneath the veneer of civility. When confronted by this "inner self," it's very easy to panic. You may even try to go back to your old way of functioning. But like Neo in The Matrix movies, once you've awakened, you can't go back. You now have to begin thinking outside the box.

So it was with me.

What I Discovered

I had what proved to be a life-changing experience—an epiphany—during my first year in graduate school, sitting among my peers in a psychopathology class. The professor was sharing case scenarios from his private practice, encouraging students in all their competitive glory to shout out the corresponding diagnoses. As I looked around the room, I noticed the expressions on many of my classmates' faces and suddenly felt mortified. My fellow students looked positively smug. This exercise in intellectual regurgitation had them feeling great about themselves, especially in relation to the "sick" individuals they were diagnosing.

These were the same students who had felt offended by an academic requirement to undertake their own personal psychotherapy sessions while attending graduate school. Psychotherapy, they reasoned, was just for "sick people." Why should *they* have to sit across from a stuffed-suit psychotherapist if they didn't think they were sick?

Visibly upset, I raised my hand and waited for the professor to call on me. I said the class had forgotten that we were talking about real people. Can you reduce a person to a label and then believe you know something genuine about that person? Can you really know what a person should look like when healthy? How do you know that the way a person's acting isn't a *healthy* response to past experiences? Is it really helpful to talk about another person in this way, as if she's sick and you, the therapist, are healthy? What about your own hidden agenda to be the authority in the room, to feel in control of another so you feel more powerful? Isn't it also true that many individuals study to become psychotherapists so they can understand their own distortions? If we're really honest with ourselves, isn't some of that almost always going on?

The professor nodded his head and said, "Yes, class, Deborah has a valid point." By the looks on their faces, however, my classmates didn't agree. Suddenly, these budding therapists were being asked to get out of their heads and feel inside themselves. It was as though they had just landed in enemy territory. For many of them, their inner landscape— the source of their beliefs and conditionings— was a place that had never seen the light of day.

I asked myself, "Would I want to tell my deepest secrets to any of these people?" The response that flooded my being was an overwhelming "Hell no!" Looking into their faces, I said, "Be careful of becoming too arrogant. Your life could change in a nanosecond, and you could find yourself sitting across from someone in our profession who wants to reduce you to a label, a problem to be solved. What then? Is that what you'd want? Is that really helpful?

"Or would it be more helpful for a therapist to validate that what you're experiencing in the moment is real for you? Wouldn't it make you feel more comfortable if the therapist was genuinely interested in your experience? Wouldn't you want to know that your therapist's motivation was one of respect and humility? With a genuine desire to support you as you were? Wouldn't you prefer a therapist who encouraged you to come to your own understanding about your experiences?"

It's easy for us to perceive how someone else functions, but it's not so easy for us to see how we function ourselves. I thought I had a valid point, but it felt like I was talking to a bunch of frightened heads that had long ago disconnected from any genuine feeling. My classmates' buried inner distortions stared me in the face. I walked out of the classroom that day with the realization that something was missing in psychotherapy—in how it's both taught and practiced. I decided then that I was going to make it my mission to find out what that was.

After-School Lessons

I've spent years exploring different modalities while trying to discover where and how psychotherapy is limited. After I graduated, I lived in Los Angeles, where nearly every modality was at my disposal, from the most advanced medical experimentation to the most outlying psychotherapeutic beliefs. I eventually crossed paths with a man who taught *bodymind integration*. (I explain this in more detail in Chapter 3.)

During my years studying with him, I came to understand another piece of the puzzle. Apparently, that big round thing sitting on our shoulders isn't a separate entity. It's somehow connected to the rest of the body, from the neck down to the toes. Everything's actually interconnected. I was intrigued. This lesson added a new dimension to my understanding of psychology:

How can psychotherapy label someone with the name of a sickness and provide analysis, but can't explain exactly "what" is going on? In other words, psychotherapists can't describe the inner mechanics of the "illness" they themselves diagnosed.

I began to realize that *why* we feel as we do is not nearly as important as *what* we feel. We don't always know why we feel the way we do and frankly, "why" just keeps us stuck in a constant loop within our overstimulated brains. That was my direct experience. To know *what* I was feeling, I had to re-learn *how* to feel. This meant I had to involve my physical body, but I didn't have a clue how or where to begin that process.

I was a psychology intern at the time, accustomed to analyzing everything. In fact, I felt proud that I could appear to know what I was doing all the time. I'd worked really hard at it. I'd studied with a few dozen therapists either as a client or as a student, so I really thought I knew my stuff.

My new bodymind integration teacher knew better. He roared with deep belly laughs at my arrogance and naïveté. He taught me that thoughts and emotions were also physical experiences. They must therefore be *felt* within the physical body. With him guiding me, I learned about the mechanics of my inner flow: the manner in which my life force or *qi* moved through me. I discovered that every one of my inner experiences corresponded to an energetic configuration. As he helped me work with the ebbs and flows of that energy, I felt my emotions—and the way I experienced myself—visibly shift.

He'd say to me, "How can you help other people come to know what they feel if *you* don't know what *you're* feeling? How can you help others track their inner experiences—the sensations, blocks, holdings, and reactions—if you can't track your own?" He'd repeat over and over, "You must always meet your clients where *they* are. So you have to acknowledge and feel your own inner experiences, moment to moment, before you can support them in feeling theirs." In other words, if I couldn't honestly feel what *I* was feeling, then I'd be too overwhelmed to see my clients as *they* were. The desire to change their experience in order to protect me from feeling mine would be too great.

I knew immediately he had a point. I had to learn more.

The Light Bulb Goes On

While with this teacher, I learned how I functioned as a person. I directly experienced how it connected to my early childhood. I cultivated the ability to feel the subtleties of that connection inside my body. More importantly, *I no longer viewed the way I functioned as a problem to be solved.* Now I was able to look at it simply as information: it told me how I functioned within myself in that particular moment. Everything within me had a valid story to tell.

This was a very different paradigm from the one I'd been taught in school. I wasn't trying to change my experience or escape it. I wasn't even trying to become healthier or improve myself. Instead, I was developing the skills to be truly honest about how I actually felt. I learned how to track and explore what I felt in the moment—mentally, emotionally, and physically—just as it was.

I began to understand that true healing always happened *within* me first. I had no idea how this new relationship with myself would manifest in my external life, but it always did, usually in a way I couldn't predict. Anytime I made plans based on where I thought I'd be later on in my process, I regretted it. By the time I actually arrived at that place, I never looked or felt the way I imagined I would. It was like laying out clothes in December for a day in March.

Each time I experienced a shift within myself, I would relate to myself differently. Simultaneously, my relationship to everyone and everything also subtly shifted, which allowed me to experience myself in relation to others differently as well. As a result, my life choices became much more effortless. I didn't have to analyze anything; my next step just became self-evident.

The key for me was to be honest with myself about my current experience and to softly and compassionately acknowledge whatever I was avoiding. This way, I could begin to *resource* myself a little at a time to consciously be with what I originally felt I couldn't. Over time, I realized I was becoming more conscious of what I was experiencing in the moment, exactly as it was. I had to keep my plans focused on the short term as much as possible since I never knew what was going to come up within me or what was going to transpire in my external life. It really was a lesson of complete surrender of my own personal agenda. My new way of functioning flowed much more naturally with the movement of my life, and this was a very different experience for me.

Ultimately, what I learned astounded me: *The way psychotherapy is taught and practiced directly contradicts the nature of true healing.* Every therapeutic exploration that takes place in a clinical office only happens between the ears. Psychotherapy does not include the physical/energetic body at all. This perspective keeps clients cycling round and round within the mental/emotional confines of their stories with no ability to re-establish a natural flow and connection within the *bodymind.*

Our pathologies are the pointers that lead us to the richest places within ourselves. In order for healing to occur, we have to move into the very root of the distortion and follow our experience, with awareness, all the way through to learn how we became identified with the thoughts, beliefs, and reactions from that time—in other words, how our previous experiences shaped the way we experience ourselves and the world. Although human beings exist on many levels, therapists and their clients ignore most of them. It's nature that does the healing as we re-establish an authentic connection with our true experience, as it is in the moment, on all levels of being. *Ultimately, all true healing happens within the soul; therefore, modern psychotherapy can only work in a limited way.*

In my new training, I re-experienced the "issues" I had already fully discussed in my earlier personal therapy sessions. I thought I had already worked through them, and yet here they were, showing up again. They just organically presented themselves as I felt the physical manifestations of my current experiences. This time, however, I wasn't *talking* about them; this time, I was *feeling* them directly. As I remained physically engaged with these "issues" I thought

I had already overcome, I began to understand how they expressed themselves in my daily life. More remarkably, I could trace the distorted way in which I functioned back to those beliefs and conditionings I was so naïvely lost to. I discovered that all the talking in the world couldn't change my internal experience.

I also engaged my inner dynamics in a very different way than I was accustomed to. It felt like the difference between expressing love directly to a person versus talking about that love to someone else. I could feel the inner expressions of my energetic flow—the blocks, holdings, and absences—shift and normalize within me. As I remained engaged with what I was feeling in each moment exactly as it was, I had no doubt that *this* was genuine healing, not an overlaid experience that felt good in the moment and mimicked quick results but didn't produce any lasting integration. As I consciously went deeper into the root of the distortion and moved all the way through it, I felt it being released from my system. I felt a natural self-correction taking place as I remained engaged with my full experience, as energetic current moved through areas that were previously blocked.

I began to feel more at ease within myself. I realized the training I'd received in my profession—teaching me to overcome my dysfunctions—didn't work. I had tried for years to overcome my "issues" by changing my external behaviors, trying to become healthier by creating new patterning within my brain. I used affirmations to desperately change my beliefs and thought patterns. This practice left me looking healthy to others but disconnected from my authentic self. Yes, I learned about myself, but not from a fuller and deeper perspective. Now I was learning to move *into and through* my experiences, just as they were, one layer at a time. This allowed them to transform and self-correct the way nature intended.

I realized then that feeling—really *feeling*—is one of the skipped steps in psychotherapy. To feel means to be directly engaged on a subtle level with *what is*. You enter the sensate world of fine feeling. Only when you have that healthy connection in place can you feel and sense your deep inner knowing with clarity. Deep healing cannot take place unless you include the physical body in your inner exploration. In fact, I later learned that you have to include all the other levels of your being as well: the mental, the emotional, and the spiritual.

This new paradigm allows you to culture and nurture an integrated physiology over time. By physiology, I mean the functioning of the body, not the structure of the anatomy. Self-awareness and healing happen degrees at a time, in an organic way. The sensations of the physiology correspond to your thoughts and emotions, but it takes confidence to be comfortable enough to tune in and honestly feel what your body experiences whenever an emotion overtakes your senses.

No wonder I'd felt so frustrated for so many years. All the inner exploration I'd done during my years of psychotherapy excluded the physical body. I hadn't, therefore, integrated my new intellectual knowledge with the other levels of my being.

Psychotherapy as it's practiced today isn't adept at effecting deep authentic healing. It's more concerned with helping people remain functional in society. While that's not a bad thing, it ignores the difference between enabling true integration and helping people function better. Integration results from cultivating a physiology that allows people to rest into themselves at deeper and deeper levels of their *whole being*. Integrated individuals follow their own natural inner rhythms, surrendered to the natural flow of life. They remain consciously engaged with their full experience exactly as it is. Integrated individuals therefore have healthier and more intimate relationships not only with themselves, but also with the nature of life and existence.

At this point in my lessons, my life took another turn. In the next part of my journey, I met another teacher who taught me about the subject of spiritual enlightenment and the ancient knowledge of Vedic science and philosophy. How is that related? Why does that matter? That's the subject of the next chapter.

CHAPTER 2

The Integration of Spirituality and Psychology

Each and every one of us is on a spiritual journey. It's impossible not to be, since everything is Spirit. Yet, there are different relationships regarding what that means to each of us. When it comes to the awakened life, many of us are so conditioned that we aren't sure what that concept *really* means to *us*. Often, we haven't spent the silent time to ponder and deeply feel for our *own* answers to the deeper questions regarding life and existence. To consciously sit with the unknown—or even with the known—can feel frightening and uncomfortable.

Yet an honest and sincere inner exploration is a valuable exercise for our personal development. If we remain honest with ourselves, we can make informed choices. There are so many different spiritual traditions, philosophies, and religions that it's difficult to make informed choices when we aren't able to consciously meet ourselves exactly as we are. To have a mature relationship with our spiritual unfolding, we must be connected to where we *genuinely* find ourselves. We can then take a deep dive inside ourselves to really inquire as to what we genuinely want to experience, as well as why we want to experience it. In other words, what are we seeking and what do we think we'll achieve if we get it?

Additionally, there are depths of awakening, so what resonates with us can also change along the way. The common thread, no matter what your phase or level of consciousness, is your honest relationship with where *you* find yourself. It's imperative to not substitute someone else's truth for your own. Reality leads us in the perfect way. It's the infinite's way of speaking to and informing us. Spiritual development is always suited to one's particular nature. It's not a question of learning something foreign to us, but of learning *ourselves*. No two natures are alike.

Having said this, for the purposes of this book and what I teach, I use the term "spirituality" in reference to the inner evolutionary process that you move through as you awaken to *the direct experience* of your true nature. This process embodies the ability to wake up from the dream of separateness to the truth of unity: that you are one with everything. But that's only the beginning. As you continue to evolve, you'll cultivate an integrated physiology through which you can actually feel the source of all life and existence as your own inner landscape. Albert Einstein called it the Unified Field. It's an act of full surrender to what is, as you wake up to the direct experience of identifying with your thoughts, beliefs, associations, ideas and reactions. *In essence, it's the process of waking up to your Transcendental nature and learning about what you're identified with and coming back down into your humanity, through the bodymind, and meeting it.*

One of my teachers used to talk about the difference between studying all about a strawberry and actually tasting the strawberry. It's fine to learn about something, as long as we know that it isn't the same thing as directly experiencing it for ourselves. However, our intellect can fool us by believing that we're directly experiencing the strawberry when we're only studying it. Therefore, the teachings in this book aren't based on any one philosophy or spiritual tradition. The focus is on our deep conscious awareness and direct physiological experience of the moment.

As you awaken more fully, you'll directly experience your true nature as the source of everything through and beyond all five senses. In other words, you'll experience yourself as pure Consciousness. At this point, you'll no longer *identify* solely with the individual expressions of your personality. This is where true wisdom is cultivated. This is where you realize how limited intellectualizations really are.

Awakening the areas within you that are conditioned expressions of who and what *you think you are* is an incredible challenge—certainly not for the faint of heart. It's an exercise in really feeling inside yourself for your full experience *as it is.* To fully realize who and *what you truly are,* you must be awake enough to discern what is and what's an expression of conditioning.

The grooves of conditioning can run deep, so this integrative process can get rough and take quite some time for some, while others may have an easier time. It requires you to be completely honest about, consciously engaged with, and 100% responsible for your internal experience. It's the difference between having an intellectual understanding of your divinity—"I think, therefore I am"—versus having a direct physiological experience of your divinity—"I am interconnected to all things."

As you pass through certain levels of development, you might find yourself drawn to different modalities at different points in your development. Allow the process to unfold organically while you discern which modality makes the most sense at the time. I ultimately discovered for myself that my relationship to any one modality either evolved my consciousness or elusively re-identified me with my conditioning.

Eastern spiritual practices teach that you are more than your personality. You aren't your thoughts or your emotions or even your physical body. Yet those aspects of yourself are expressions of your individual relationship to your whole being—mentally, emotionally, physically, and spiritually. That's the allure of the spiritual path.

My Private Ashram

In my quest to find the missing piece of psychotherapy and awaken myself spiritually, I spent well over a decade learning about the process of healing while feeling and exploring my inner terrain on deeper and deeper levels. For many of those years, I isolated myself from the collective world that we normally all share. Whatever I experienced, I wanted to feel it fully and honestly as it was in the moment without changing it. It took a lot of focus and practice just to do this one "simple" thing.

In essence, you could say that I created my own private ashram. I devoted myself completely to developing self-awareness. I was newly married, but fortunately, my partner supported and honored my path. The love and safety of my marriage seemed to speed up my process, as if the floodgates organically opened and I could no longer hide from any experience within myself.

I admit it wasn't a conventional path for a Westerner to take, but since I didn't aspire to go to a formal ashram, I created my own program. I worked with my bodymind integration teacher weekly by phone, and my husband offered his services as a holistic health practitioner—a Chinese herbalist, acupuncturist, and body worker. I also followed an Ayurvedic diet and lifestyle, lived in a small home near the beach, and used most of my savings to create a healing environment.

In retrospect, I had no clue what I'd set in motion. I just knew deep in my soul that I wanted to directly experience and live from my true nature no matter what the consequences. And trust me, there were many consequences. But the experience was an insignificant price to pay for the clarity and authenticity I enjoy today.

So there I was, married and living an ashram lifestyle, while I remained committed to exploring *what is* on all levels of my being. I moved into deeper and subtler levels of feeling while waking up to the incarnate mappings of my core belief. This organically led me into a direct relationship with undeveloped infantile aspects within myself, as well as other incomplete stages of my early childhood development. In other words, I found that part of my energy was stuck in a time loop in which I kept repeating experiences I'd had as a child over and over. I didn't experience these mappings from the experience of the integrated whole. I experienced them as subtle nuances, cloaked in charge, that felt like disembodied and isolated fragments that did not have the luxury of being part of the totality of my being. I sat in silence every day for hours, physically tracking, feeling, and observing my relationship to my thoughts, reactions, associations, beliefs, identities, and energetic flow. Since my deepest motivation was to have a direct experience of my true nature, I had to consciously engage my early childhood distortions as they organically presented themselves. This was incredibly challenging because while I had talked about my early childhood experiences, I hadn't physically felt them all the way through to completion until now.

Once I made a conscious choice to remain honestly engaged with my experience exactly as it was, something within began to relax. As a result, experiences that had been repressed, suppressed, and seemingly overcome began to move up into my awareness. It took me some time to effortlessly move with what organically presented itself.

By learning this, I hoped to better understand how healing truly happens. In my private practice as a psychotherapist, I'd witnessed so much suffering. Yet I didn't resonate with the limited way in which I'd been taught to work with my clients. Nor could I settle for the limited way in which my previous personal therapists and teachers had worked with me. All the theories and philosophies I'd studied weren't enough to affect the direct experience of deep healing and awakening I desired. I just couldn't believe the notion that once you were an addict, you'd always be an addict. It didn't make sense that once you were diagnosed as being bi-polar, you would always have an experience of being bi-polar. Something was still missing.

So every day, I tracked what I was feeling—my emotions as well as my physical sensations, which were expressions of my inner energetic flow. Initially, this practice was to simply observe what I was experiencing within myself and to witness the inner workings of my beliefs, such as how I identified with my distortions. I admit this was a huge challenge for me. The desire to change my experience was very strong. To stay with my experience *as it was* felt daunting because I had conditioned myself to stop feeling anything that was uncomfortable. But I persevered because deep inside I could connect the dots and directly feel that my discomfort was an expression of my beliefs.

As I tracked my inner reactions day to day, I became aware of what my bodymind integration teacher meant when he said, *"Every emotional experience has a corresponding energetic signature."* When I moved my body in a specific way to allow the energetic flow to normalize, it changed how I experienced myself. I hadn't talked about anything; I had allowed my inner flow to restore itself by bringing my awareness to my energetic configuration. Then I noticed that my relationship to whatever experience I was resisting also began to change. In essence, I was doing my own yoga. I could feel where the inner blocks and holdings were, and I found ways to work with my physical body that allowed them to self-correct a little at a time.

For example, if I was experiencing fear, I'd feel within myself and notice that the energetic flow in my left leg felt constricted, as though it lacked full physical presence. If I did something as basic as bring my awareness to my left big toe while feeling the subtleties of the sensation (or lack thereof), I could literally feel the blood flow move down into that leg. Then I'd experience my leg as having more substance. I realized that simultaneously, my relationship to the earlier fear changed profoundly, yet very subtly. In this example, the lack of flow in my left leg expressed my beliefs and conditionings, by which I mean my reactions to those beliefs and conditionings. That may seem like a giant leap, but it's true.

Let me explain: In nature, everything is interconnected, so everything affects everything else. A thought can trigger a physical or emotional reaction that comes from a past association with our beliefs. This unconscious reaction in turn becomes an experience that we identify as who and what we are. This energetic distortion is how we keep from having an experience that's too intense, but it comes at a price. Our beliefs and our highly charged reactions get mapped throughout our physiology; therefore, an absence in the leg produces a response throughout the body, as well as on other levels of our being. Working with the specifics of our energetic flow creates the potential for us to develop a more conscious understanding of our relationship to the beliefs and conditionings from which we function. This process also gives us the ability to work *directly* with our inner charges.

I experienced myself—my whole being: physical, mental, emotional, spiritual, and psychological—with much more clarity. I didn't have to force my energy in any one direction. I just observed how it flowed and then noted what specific reactions it prompted. This gave me an ongoing understanding of my inner mechanics; it provided me with the beginnings of a map of my inner landscape. This understanding changed my relationship toward my reactive behavior. I finally understood how a feeling could innocently overtake me. That's what happens.

I also learned that there's an art in determining which course of action to take. Which level of my being should I explore to potentially bring about the most healing? Should

I begin by talking about my experience? Should I feel inward to track my energetic flow? How about feeling into and observing my blocked or knotted-up energy (that is, my inner holdings)? At first, these questions felt awkward. But over time, I cultivated an ability to truly and honestly *feel*, so I could determine within myself how best to proceed.

Another Course of Study: Vedic Knowledge

As the years passed, I realized it was time for me to venture back out into the world. Not long after this decision, I found another teacher. This teacher had established a formal school in which he lectured on the subjects of spiritual enlightenment and healing, so it seemed a perfect match for what I'd been studying thus far.

This also gave me the opportunity to interact with other people, which wasn't what I was used to. After the years of inner work in my own private ashram, my physiology was accustomed to silence, reflection, and isolation. Re-entering the world was a shock to my system. But I did it, a little at a time, since instinctively I felt it was the right thing at the right time. I needed to further integrate all the work I'd done within myself as I re-experienced the outside world. This way, I could see where I was getting caught in my own reactivity as I interacted with others.

I continued one-on-one weekly phone sessions with my bodymind integration teacher, but now I added four well-attended, intensive classes per year with my new teacher, plus two week-long meditation retreats. At this point in my inner development, this specific teacher (and his school) was the right fit for me. His lessons involved learning and experiencing the nature of existence from an ancient Vedic perspective in order to cultivate a physiological state of enlightenment. In Eastern traditions such as this one, the Veda is considered to be the source of all Knowledge.

Back when I'd lived in Los Angeles, I'd been introduced to meditation and the spiritual teachings of a very popular and famous enlightened master from India. I had enjoyed these studies immensely, so I was thrilled to learn my new teacher had lived in the master's ashram in India for many years as his student. He understood the value of personal process and incorporated his own unique perspective on the subject in his teachings. I knew this would complement the work I was already doing. Moreover, he taught hands-on healing. Since I'd already learned how to work with my energetic flow to bring about organic healing and self-awareness through my own direct experience and from my bodymind integration teacher, I eagerly learned his perspective.

By returning to the world, I found and studied with a new teacher. This period introduced the next stage of my healing and inner development work. As a result, I learned about another piece of the puzzle: spirituality and its role in healing.

Why Psychotherapy Still Matters

While we may indeed be spiritual beings, we are indeed having a human experience. Some spiritual teachings don't even mention the practice of exploring and integrating the personality. This creates a distortion within our individual experience of ourselves by limiting the degree to which we can fully experience our true nature. Can we really fully embrace the divine if we're still caught up in the conditioning from our childhood experiences?

If we avoid or stifle the unique expressions of our personalities, our egos don't develop properly, which can keep us caught in our inner reactions, living from our history instead of from our present. This can override the human experience, leaving a gap in our human and psychological development.

It's been my experience that the true spiritual path isn't just about awakening to the divine, but also about seamlessly integrating our whole being, which includes the personality, the emotions, the bodymind, and the ego—in other words, awakening to our universality, as well as to our individual expression of divinity. This includes the conscious ascending, as well as the descending, expression of Spirit. The allure of psychology, on the other hand, is its ability to understand the psyche and map out a path for us to develop healthy egos. Psychology makes it possible for us to understand the mechanics of the personality.

The Intersection Between Psychology and Spirituality

Both psychotherapeutic explorations and a spiritual practice—in their very different perspectives and methodologies—have value. In exploring one, you always encounter the other. It's impossible to awaken to the spiritual expression of Self without simultaneously facing the individual expression of your psychology. They are interconnected; you cannot have one without the other. If you try to ignore one, it limits your experience of your whole being. This incomplete expression of Self is a result of trying to experience your true nature from of a limited perspective, like trying to see the Grand Canyon through a peephole.

There has to be wisdom in how we integrate the study and exploration of both spirituality and the psychology of the individual. We can experientially bring these two perspectives together seamlessly within our conscious awareness, resulting in an integrative experience that connects the dots rather than isolating them. It's possible to consciously validate our individual experiences and stories without unconsciously reinforcing them. We are not our stories; our true being expands beyond them.

We cannot use a piecemeal approach to do this. That's repeatedly been tried, and it doesn't work. There are many quick fixes and out-in approaches to financial prosperity, spiritual development, and mental health. Each tells us how, in ten or twelve steps, we can obtain abundance, enlightenment, or healing. We're sold on the notion that we can control our minds and our lives to have the results we think we want. Usually, we begin optimistically, seeking signs that we're making progress. Then one day, we have to admit it isn't working for us any longer. We forgot to keep our positive thoughts in place, or we just feel depressed and exhausted from having to try so hard. Yet when we try to avoid our experience of the moment and tell nature how we think our experience should be, not only do we create an inner divide, but we also don't allow our soul to have the experiences needed to evolve our consciousness. Most of us have done the best we can, but as a result, we've had to compromise the very thing we're trying to achieve: the natural unfolding of our essential selves—because true healing is *the organic unveiling of who and what we truly are.*

The Deep Grooves of Conditioning

For some of us, it's chic to be "spiritual." We like the communal feeling we get from following a certain faith or religious philosophy. We might think being on a spiritual path makes us look "cool" or "together." But the concept of spirituality can easily become a trap, another persona or identity to cling to, another thing to keep us from feeling our experience exactly as it is and to avoid what we fear most.

The way to deep healing, awakening, and *whole-istic* integration is a deep and profound path. You can't know what lies ahead when you begin this journey. Your perception of life and existence is profoundly limited when you're unconsciously caught in and functioning from your deepest conditioning. However, if you're called to live what's real, true, and authentic, you'll ultimately surrender and take that dive inward. Not because it makes you more special to be awake, but because being awake and clear is our natural state—although it's uncommon in this era.

It's important to note, however, that the process of honestly acknowledging your current experience and surrendering to the natural flow of life doesn't necessarily make you feel better, happier, or more comfortable—especially in the beginning. Most everyone fights reality in some way and at some point within the evolutionary process. This resistance brings suffering with it. My Vedic teacher used to say to me, "You come to *nirvana* by way of *samsara*." The way you function, therefore, isn't something to be ashamed of or denied. In fact, it's your gateway to truth, if you use it wisely.

As you wake up to your divinity, you directly experience your true nature on deeper and fuller levels. You ultimately feel it seamlessly integrated throughout your physiology. As I said earlier, the journey inward looks uniquely different for everyone. It doesn't come with a manual; therefore, it can be intimidating to individuals that have become wired to analyze, change, or fix their experience. Just as I was.

The key component of these teachings is to effortlessly and wisely move with nature. By moving inward and surrendering to what is, exactly as it is, while remaining conscious on all levels of being, you're able to witness and feel your story—in all its expressions—unfold. These expressions show up as physical and energetic holdings and blockages that come from unconscious reactions to and motivations from past experiences, identification with the story, thoughts patterns, and belief systems. As your relationship to your inner terrain becomes honest and direct, your consciousness evolves and you cultivate wisdom. Through this unfolding, your relationship to everything changes. It's impossible to continue unconsciously functioning from the same artificial persona when you're really honest with yourself about your inner experiences in all their subtleties.

As your relationship to your previously distorted modes of function destabilize, you'll simultaneously begin to feel a broader and deeper perspective *awaken you.* You might not think destabilization is part of the spiritual path, but it is, very much. Destabilization occurs as you awaken, experience a spontaneous shift of identity, and cultivate a direct physiological experience of your true nature. As a result, the life you've created for yourself will most likely change in some manner as you actualize, since your life was formed out of your conditioned point of view. *As your inner resonance shifts, your external environment follows.*

Developing a healthy relationship with your outer world *exactly as it is* is crucial. *You awaken to where you are, not where you think you should be.* This includes your relationship with others, such as your parents, friends, siblings, co-workers, and spouses. It's important to give all your relationships some time and space to organically evolve, as you reflect on your relationship to yourself, as well as how you currently relate to others.

For instance, as a child, you're completely dependent upon your caregivers. If your experience of yourself becomes chronically distorted in those early years, it can have a profound effect on your psychological development. Early life traumas can set you up for a lifetime of conditioning that can't self-correct just by talking about them. For these deeper grooves to naturally heal, you might need to explore and feel their current expression through the multiple layers all the way to their point of origin. This experiential process can create the proper conditions for distortions to self-correct while they release themselves from your system. Additionally, as your system recalibrates, you'll have to learn to accommodate new energetic flow moving through previously blocked areas of your body and to experience the psycho-physiological updating of your early childhood experiences.

You also have to look and feel deeply enough while considering multiple perspectives in your inner exploration. Exploring your current experience from different perspectives evolves your consciousness and frees you from your conditioning. For example, you're born to parents who are right for you and who give you the experiences that can potentially help awaken you, so you can engage your core belief. Therefore, when you explore your inner landscape from this perspective, your childhood experiences can give you an abundant amount of information since they are expressions of the beliefs you function from. It's important to include the whole picture so you can gain deeper clarity. Looking and feeling deeply allows you to take full responsibility for your experiences so you can learn what you're meant to learn from them.

It's similar to the analogy that your life and the individuals in it represent a script that you wrote, including its themes and many roles. This is *your* story. You have cast individuals to play their roles in order to bring life to your story so you can have a specific experience. In order to enter into a fuller relationship with yourself and learn from your experiences, you'll want to develop a conscious relationship with your script so you can wake up and experientially connect the dots to realize that *you* have authored the screenplay and cast the roles. Therefore, the popular saying, "don't kill the messenger," applies here. As I said earlier, it's not possible to separate the study of psychology from that of spirituality. They are interconnected.

Another dilemma is finding the right facilitator. The problem is this: not many psychotherapists have done inner development work that organically includes their whole being, and not many spiritual teachers include personal process and psychology as part of their teachings. Furthermore, few therapists have integrated their physiology to the point that they've consciously surrendered to the natural flow of life, and few Eastern gurus believe in the value of psychotherapy, since their primary focus is on the higher realms of existence.

How can you solve this problem? Ultimately, you must take responsibility for your own evolution. Take the time to wisely choose the tools, modalities, and facilitators to support you in your inner development. Psychotherapists and spiritual teachers help tremendously, but for this endeavor to be successful, you must learn to think and discern for yourself. Become your own teacher. All worthwhile teachings point you back to yourself anyway. Teachings mean very little if you never have the experience for yourself. You can't just learn; you have to learn to do it for yourself. This path takes you beyond the illusion of control. This means you have to cultivate wisdom, the art of subtle feeling, and an informed way of moving inward—which is the subject of the next chapter.

CHAPTER 3

The Body and the Mind Are Not Separate

Sensations, emotions, and thoughts add up to feelings. Yet feelings and emotions aren't meant to define us. Whether joyful or painful, they are simply meant to be felt. Feelings and sensations are where the incarnated soul experiences and expresses itself. The more comfortable we are with our physical, mental, and emotional experience of ourselves, the more fully incarnated we are. However, in our culture, most of us aren't taught *how* to truly feel. The best we can do is intellectualize our inner experiences, which is definitely not the same as *physically feeling* those experiences.

When you resist reality as it is, you create a distortion in your physical, energetic, and psychological flow. I call this distortion a block, absence, or holding. As stress accumulates within your physiology, distortions can cause physical illness and even mental and emotional imbalance. Living your distortions creates a disconnect within the *bodymind* that renders you unable to follow your natural inner rhythms. Just as everything is interconnected in nature, so too are the body and mind interconnected. There is no separation between them. In essence, they are one.

If you're not able to remain consciously engaged with what you genuinely *feel* on multiple levels, you can end up living day-by-day in an unconscious or semi-conscious mode—seemingly safe behind multiple masks, roles, or personas. To fool yourself, you compensate by doing what you "think" will be acceptable to others as a means to diminish your charge, and therefore the discomfort, of your own inner distress. This distorted mode of function instills a split within the bodymind, keeping the natural harmonization of thinking and feeling impeded; yet more importantly, it's also keeping you from feeling what you *believe* you cannot consciously feel. That's its value.

If you can view this from the perspective that you are a co-creator of your life, then "this way of functioning" provides a window into your patterns of conditioning that you want to awaken to, as opposed to overcome or fix. It's a valid and valuable piece of the puzzle that points you back to your innate wholeness.

Feeling Things as They Are

When you lose touch with what you authentically feel in the moment, the best you can do is follow someone else's interpretation of your experience. Whether you go to a psychotherapist or read the latest self-help book or try a new diet, you try to find the modality—the interpretation—that appeals to you the most at that particular time.

This way of functioning keeps you looking to others as a way to validate your current experience of yourself and to help diminish the distress you chronically experience. No matter how many expert opinions you obtain, though, it will never be a substitute for your direct connection to yourself. Feeling your experience exactly as it is allows your stories to be told to yourself, by yourself and through yourself. This is where all your transformations will take place.

For example, if you can't physically, emotionally, and psychologically accommodate what you feel, you have to *go unconscious* to cut yourself off from what you're currently experiencing. Your body has wisdom, and that wisdom protects you. If an experience feels like it's too much for you to handle, the bodymind finds a way to dampen your reaction—even if it has to separate you from the experience. This is called survival. Denial exists to help you survive. Similarly, you wouldn't think of prying a person's eyes open to see something you know he would deny. That's called torture. *Prying people's eyes and ears open doesn't create a healthier relationship with an experience or with themselves.* It merely furthers the distortions within their bodymind.

On the other hand, when you heal naturally, you organically arrive at the next place or layer within where you can engage yourself without prodding from an outside source. Stopping a behavior or pattern of thinking isn't the same as consciously understanding your relationship to it. If the internal mechanics that determine and drive how you function remain the same, which occurs when you try an outside-in remedy, you'll likely pick up the behavior again or find a different behavior that allows you to unconsciously diminish the same internalized charge.

Instead of encouraging that vicious cycle, the inner work I recommend teaches you to consciously diminish the intensity so you can accommodate your developing inner experience, layer upon layer. This way, you integrate all levels of being a little at a time, learning what you can and cannot accommodate as you go. This brings about deep healing in as safe a manner as possible.

The key is to have a healthy flow—a healthy give and take—between thinking and feeling. It's important to be able to do both. *Feeling* asks you to get in touch with your physiological expression, the subtle world of sensation. When you *feel,* you don't try to figure anything out. Instead, you just quiet yourself and let the feeling tell the story. You move into a deep state of listening. The body has its own story, and it's usually very different from the story you'll hear from your overstimulated brain.

Our thoughts often *seem* so imperative that we end up *thinking* our way through our life experiences. Thinking cut off from physically feeling, however, encourages even more thinking, which continues until our brain enters a cycle that loops endlessly. The more energy caught up in this loop, the more we try to figure it out. The brain has to do something with the excess energy generated when we're caught up in our intellect, so it spins out. This way of functioning can cause us to become chronic over-analyzers or over-intellectualizers. A few examples of this inner dynamic are "worrywarts," people who talk quickly or incessantly, and people who over analyze themselves and others.

In my opinion, *feeling is the missed step in our culture.* It's a big reason we've lost our ability to access our inner knowing. Feeling allows us to be honest with ourselves on a deeper level.

Natural Healing

We have wired ourselves to override our *actual* inner experience so our belief system remains unchallenged. We believe that if we can change or *overcome* our current thinking that led to certain perceived unhealthy behaviors, then we have become healthier. This is the impetus behind outside-inside models and techniques such as cognitive behavioral therapy, as well as the positivity movement that affirms positive thinking by letting you pick and choose your preferred thoughts. One example of this behavior is affirming daily that you are safe in this world and connected to everything. In this situation, you actually *feel* unsafe in the world and disconnected from yourself, but you're trying to tell yourself to feel differently. Since your reality is too overwhelming to feel honestly within yourself, you seek to change your experience. Yet does it really change or have you just disconnected from it so you won't feel it with the same intensity? Just because you've stopped feeling something or transcended it doesn't mean it's been resolved or eradicated. It's still endlessly wreaking havoc on your system. You can't consciously connect the dots to understand that this is why you experience the pathology, the reactivity, and the deep disconnect within yourself. Until you can consciously meet yourself—with all your experiences exactly as they are—and validate all the stories within the larger context of who and what you "truly are," your inner configuration will stay the same.

I've found from my own direct experience that if the charge is too great, you'll avoid the very place inside yourself you need to compassionately acknowledge, feel, open to and move through in order to evolve your consciousness so a natural correction can take place. You therefore must become proficient at working with and diminishing the intensity of your inner charge so you can be with your full experience more comfortably and with clarity, so you can learn what you need to learn from that experience.

True empowerment comes from living truthfully and authentically, surrendered to the natural flow of life. To do this, you'll need to take an inward journey to explore, feel, and observe your inner terrain with tremendous honesty, sincerity, and discernment. Since you exist on many levels, you'll also want to cultivate a healthy relationship with each level to bring about a seamless integration. You'll be better able to accommodate what you feel and experience as your relationship to the distortions you carry self-corrects degrees at a time.

My experience suggests that our brain patterns can't change by simply changing our behaviors. The deep grooves we've dug are the result of our deeply held beliefs. We've been digging these grooves for many years, possibly most of our lives. They aren't superficial tracks, and they won't necessarily self-correct easily, certainly not by repeating a few words every day. There is value, however, in temporarily creating new behaviors if your current behavioral patterns put you or someone else in danger. Just remember that this change isn't a cure; it's a skipped step. To really heal the unhealthy behavior, you eventually have to remain engaged with your current experience as it is, so you can become resourced differently, internally and externally. Then you can consciously track and feel your reactions as you move through your experience in a way that was impossible when the deep distortion was originally created.

Some of the most famous self-help teachers and authors often teach that if you affirm your desired outcome and really believe it, you'll create new patterning within your mind to manifest your new belief. This type of teaching, though, removes you from your natural inner rhythms. It's a shortcut to a preferred outcome that interrupts the natural flow and momentum of deep healing and integration. It's not the belief, but your *relationship* to the belief that shifts over time. That's my biggest issue with positive thinking and affirmations, as well as the use of certain techniques through which we attempt to create the states of being that we want to experience.

And yet: what if what we *think* we want is coming from the impetus of conditioning? Not to mention: if we're trying to change our experience, how can our soul have the experience it needs in order to learn what it's meant to learn? Until we cultivate a deeper and wiser relationship to life and existence, we'll be led astray by our constant search for superficial quick fixes that carry fragmented elements of truth. The real truth is that it's impossible not to have experiences in life that challenge us and don't feel good. Life can be brutal and gritty. Once we make peace with that fact and learn how to wisely move with our life experience, we suffer much less. Enlightenment—or awakening—isn't a panacea.

I do, however, use affirmations or visualizations in my work as a means to trigger whatever reactive expressions of the belief is next in line for you to witness and engage. This can give you more information about your relationship to the beliefs from which you're currently functioning, as well as whether you've released the distortion fully from your system. For example, if you feel frightened of being alone, allow yourself to imagine being alone and notice what within you feels triggered. If you don't have the skill set to work this directly, however, then give yourself the time to safely cultivate it.

The point is that you can't heal yourself simply by telling yourself you shouldn't be having the thoughts you're having. Trying to change your thoughts is just a superficial manipulation of a much deeper distortion you carry within. Once you can directly experience that *you* aren't your thoughts or emotions—and you've integrated this awareness on all levels of your being—you won't have to override or manipulate those thoughts or emotions. They simply won't have the same hold on you any longer. One of my teachers once told me that your relationship with your thoughts—how you feel about them—is much more important than the thoughts themselves. That relationship drives how you act and react.

You can look at your thoughts from multiple perspectives. From an energetic perspective, a thought is a natural expression of your energetic flow as it moves through your brain. It can be called a *brain sensation*. Uncontrollable thoughts can be an expression of too much rising energy rushing into your brain. When energy gets stuck in your upper body, it becomes backlogged and overstimulates your brain. If you try to examine these thoughts, you can get caught up in them, creating an energy loop in your brain that just keeps cycling within itself. If you try to ignore the thoughts, you can create a further distortion within your energy system. Needless to say, this condition does not allow you to function from your true nature. All it does is cause confusion about who and what you *think* you are.

The Process of Healing

In nature, healing happens when you align yourself with what you're feeling moment to moment, exactly as it is. You don't have to change your inner experience. You don't have to force yourself in any one direction. At the same time, you can't avoid the experience either. You have to acknowledge what it is you're experiencing and how it's affecting you without trying to fix it.

Natural healing happens within that "window." It happens on the inside first. It happens degrees at a time, layer upon layer, with no preconceived notion of what the result should look like. This is how you reconnect to the natural rhythms within yourself.

Living your life in accord with natural law heals your inner distortions. In time, your outer life comes to reflect your internal changes. You start to see and feel the natural, organic relationship that develops between your inner and outer worlds. You begin to live authentically, directly experiencing your whole being. You don't transcend whatever you feel frightened of. You feel not just connected, but *inter*connected with all the levels of your being—mental, emotional, physical, and spiritual.

Exploring one component of your being has an effect on how you experience yourself on other levels as well. For example, if you feel a specific pain behind your forehead, you might feel into that area of the brain. Sometimes, nothing happens. You might notice, however, that as you explore a block you feel in your solar plexus, your headache diminishes. Everything affects everything else.

The necessary inner work, therefore, must incorporate

your *Whole Being*. Every level (mental, emotional, physical, and spiritual) must become part of your self-exploration. It's not enough—and it's not effective—to merely explore your thoughts. You must explore your relationships with your thoughts, your beliefs, your motivations, your physical sensations, and even your identities. Discovering that you've *identified with*—and currently experience yourself as—your beliefs, thought patterns, and inner reactions becomes a lively and organic roadmap for integrating all the levels of your being. Consciously working with your relationship to these thoughts and reactions leads to healthy relationships with yourself, with others, and with the world at large.

Being with your inner experience as it is can feel very challenging to your *identities*—the mapped expressions of your self-limiting beliefs and conditionings. These identities have a job to do, and they aren't going to necessarily give up easily. Yet when a certain place or construct within you is enlivened, it so strongly feels like who and what you are, you'd swear that's what it is. After all, that's your current experience of yourself.

It's a fact that you feel what you feel. It isn't productive, therefore, to talk yourself out of what you feel. This only serves to invalidate you. It's much more effective to validate that the experiences *are real for you*. Then you can begin to explore your relationship to those experiences.

There's an art to this type of work, and it takes time and practice to learn. Therapists and facilitators have to meet you where you are. They have to work with you in *the moment exactly as it is,* while allowing you to track what you feel internally and without letting you get too caught up in it. Therapists and facilitators must recognize that you might have identified exclusively with the enlivened experience to the point that it feels like who and what you are. If you feel too overwhelmed, you'll go *unconscious* and won't be able to stay present with the experience, which reduces the likelihood that any type of natural self-correction will take place. Consciously experiencing how you function from your conditioning allows you to awaken to your current inner dynamic with clarity. For therapists and facilitators, this inner exploration is the key to evolving your consciousness and rewiring your physiology.

If you're like most people, you've become accustomed to using healing modalities (usually from outside ourselves) that create an artificial and superficial disruption of your currently held beliefs and distortions. Since these changes happen quickly, they've tainted your expectations so that you're now used to immediate results. Yet these changes aren't true changes in the sense that they are deep and lasting. Superficial changes don't allow your inner distortions to unfold naturally. They don't facilitate organic healing and integration.

Healing is an unfathomable process with all its complex subtleties, especially if trauma is involved. Each layer in your healing process reveals a new relationship to the whole and a new expression of energetic holdings or mappings within your physiology. If you don't resist any part of your experience, then healing can become much simpler, yet this isn't necessarily the same thing as feeling good. As you compassionately embrace and reclaim all the energies and lost and isolated aspects of your being within, they find validation for their existence and the newfound freedom to awaken and integrate back into the whole.

This process delivers you into a different relationship with yourself and your currently held beliefs. In other words, you don't "fix" your issues; instead, you feel them as *part of* your experience. They aren't the whole of you, but they are part of how you currently experience yourself. Really knowing this makes it possible for you to remain engaged with them on a conscious level since you wake up *within* your distortion, not beyond it. *Your internal experience of fear will always lead you to where you need self-care.* You might need to find a qualified practitioner to support you while you're moving into and through your experience as it actually is, so you can remain conscious and thus become more comfortable with your inner dynamic.

Beginning the Journey

The integrative work I share throughout this book is part of a grounded approach that naturally brings us *deeper inside ourselves*. True healing happens from the inside first and then trickles outward into our daily lives. So many people try to start from where they want to be or think they should be. That path leads, ultimately, to disappointment. We cannot be someplace before we genuinely arrive. So we begin our journey from right where we are in this moment. Where else can we expect to start?

To live authentically means to live honestly, to live what's real. We truly believe that we *are* the things we most fear. So we do whatever we can—whatever it takes—to deny it, repress it, suppress it, avoid it, and override it. Consciously (or more often, unconsciously), we're determined to prove to ourselves that we aren't the things we fear we are. As a result, we look everywhere for answers except in the place we need to look, the place inside that counts the most.

To compensate, we jump from one knot to the next, from one external quick fix to another, hoping this one will finally resolve the issues we have with our body image, our addictive behaviors, our fears, our anxieties, our compulsions, our illnesses . . . the list goes on and on. When we discover, in the long run, that the solution we've chosen isn't the answer we thought it was, we go looking for the next quick fix, like a self-help junkie. We desperately crave that magic spell or affirmation that changes everything, that one thing to help us not have to go *there,* that modality or theory that helps us feel better about ourselves and stops our destructive, abusive, or self-defeating behaviors. Any of this sound familiar?

Most of us try just about everything before we exhaust our resources and ultimately surrender. At that moment, we realize the truth: that we feel as we do, we function as we do, and we behave as we do. That's the reality. This inner experience, however, in no way reflects who and what we really are. This is just a road map that says, "You are here."

Congratulations. You've just arrived at The Present Tense. It often doesn't look as good or as bad as you probably thought it would. It's from this place that you begin the journey inward toward "yourself," meaning your *True* Self.

The First Steps

Your evolutionary process is not linear. Healing is like unraveling a knotted, delicate gold chain. Pull the knot of chain in one direction, and there's no way to know which part of the chain will unravel and which part will knot up again, often in a different way. You must pay attention and progress with care. You can't force the knot to unravel. It's a delicate process.

Similarly, you have to feel and track each of your inner layers as it moves into a new relationship with your established beliefs and identities. To do this, you engage what is in front of you just as it is.

When you function from your conditioning, your perception of yourself is narrowed, almost like you have tunnel vision, and you *identify* with the story and its particulars. Because the experience feels so intense, you begin to think and believe it's who and what you are. You believe it so fervently that it distorts your perception. You've structured your reactions in such a specific way that it feels very real. This reactivity feels so unsettling that you do everything you can to keep yourself from having that experience again. Nature, however, has a different plan.

Exploring Through the Layers

Your physical body is an expression or map of your core story. As you track and feel into the subtle expressions of your current energetic configuration, through the internalized blocks and holdings, you create the potential for each layer to self-correct and reconfigure itself. Your energetic flow is described as your life force, *qi,* or *prana.* Many channels of flow move through your body. Yet, the main channel of flow moves up from the earth into your feet, through your legs, up through the center, out of the top of your head, and back around again. Simultaneously, another flow moves from the heavens into the top of your head, through the center of the body, down through your legs and feet, and back around again. You live in a world of duality, and your energetic flow is no different.

Your flowing energy creates a type of field. This level of being is a rich area for exploration and healing. Illnesses and imbalances show up here as blocks and holdings. As you explore them, you can find an entry into the stories being expressed through your physical and energetic bodies by consciously feeling and witnessing your current experience. Since everything is interconnected, you have the potential to clear up distortions on the physical, mental, and emotional levels through this single exploration of the energetic level. Wisdom is feeling and sensing which level of your being to engage in any given moment to bring about the most healing within yourself.

It's crucial, therefore, to have a grounded understanding of the mechanics of nature and existence. This knowledge serves as the basis for all the healing that takes place, giving you a foundation from which to develop. You can't go wrong if you consciously stay moment-to-moment with what you feel within yourself, just as it is, while naturally and effortlessly flowing with the inner and outer movement of life. Take it one step—one stage—at a time.

One important note: the rules of one level of existence don't necessarily apply to another. In other words, they don't carry over or cross boundaries. Each level has its own laws. For example, on the spiritual level of your being, there is no such thing as death or time. You are pure, absolute consciousness. Yet on the emotional level, you can experience feelings about death—your own or someone else's. If who and what you truly are is pure, absolute consciousness, then there is no such thing as death. Then why have feelings about it? You have feelings because part of your existence is expressed on the physical and emotional levels. That's why the loss of a loved one can feel painful.

Yet the spiritual plane and the emotional plane have very different expressions. Both must be respected for their unique natures. When you have an integrated awareness of both levels, you'll be able to feel them simultaneously as your authentic experience without feeling it as a contradiction. Through the integrative process, you'll cultivate a physiological ability to move with wisdom and ease from one level to the next while remembering the differences. So while the loss of a loved one can feel emotionally painful, you let yourself feel it while also feeling a direct experience of the transcendental quality of your nature. Both things are true and yet they're experienced differently.

The Infant Bodymind

Consciously feeling your physical body, moment-to-moment, and tracking the physical expression of your thought patterns and emotions can help you integrate your physiology with any incomplete childhood developmental stages mapped onto the structures of the personality. Since your body is a repository of stuck emotions, it acts as an important resource to help you understand and consciously work within the very primitive expression of your *infant bodymind*.

The infant bodymind is an imprinting of the infant/child experiences that got mapped onto the physiology during your early childhood developmental stages. This imprinting can be a very intense charge if your early years were met with fear, terror, engulfment, attack, neglect, or disengagement with your caregiver. When infants experience trauma, it leaves them outwardly focused and inwardly unaware. This internal reaction maps onto their developmental timeline and their physiologies, which is why healing infant trauma can be a long and uncomfortable journey. I'll discuss this very important concept in further detail in Chapter 7.

Working consciously with the infant bodymind enables you to move into a healthier relationship with the childhood patterns you adopted. These patterns, which once served as a way to help you endure or survive, now keep you functioning in a limited and limiting way. Healing this inner dynamic involves your ability to move into a more emotionally and spiritually mature relationship with yourself, one in which you live in harmony with your true nature—who and what you *really* are. You gradually move from "survive" to "thrive."

This process includes being in the moment with your past history: not denying it or avoiding it, but moving into acceptance of what has happened and is happening in the moment within you. As you lean in this direction, you'll be less caught up by your past reactions and associations and more able to be in the ever-present moment as it is.

Your past gives you your individual, unique perceptions. Your past gives you your history. These things cannot change. What *will* change is your perception of the past. That "little" shift can free you so that your past no longer defines you. That is a real step forward in your personal evolution.

What does all this have to do with healing? What does it mean to truly heal? How can you move toward true healing? How can you live what's authentic and real? It's up to you to take the first steps toward discovering these answers. My goal is to validate and support you as you begin to experience the paradigm shift that will occur within the inner workings of your consciousness.

CHAPTER 4

Complete Honesty

Most people feel intimidated by the prospect of beginning their inner self-exploration. Where do you start? The basic rule of thumb is to *begin with what you're experiencing in the current moment, exactly as it is, on whatever level of your being you experience it.* Be honest with yourself about what you feel inside without editing anything.

For instance, if you're feeling frightened, acknowledge that the fear is a *feeling* (an actual *physical sensation*) that you call "fear." Then let yourself consciously open to it. Feel how your body experiences the sense of fear. Where in your body does it manifest itself? Don't force an answer or response. Allow it to be what it is. If there is resistance, accept it and be with the resistance. If information comes flooding forward, let yourself *be* with that.

Any time you experience sensation, it always produces a thought as energy moves upward through the brain. The greater the charge you carry, the more intense your experience will be. As flow surges upward and hits the brain, it produces a myriad of thoughts. If you're not paying attention, your awareness of yourself gets unconsciously carried into the uncontrollable thoughts. Becoming experienced with the particulars of how flow moves through a physiology is an important tool to have, so you can successfully *wake up* within your story.

When doing the inner exploration work, it's important to do your best to not jump to conclusions about your experience. It's common to feel overwhelmed at first. You're becoming aware of how lost you really are to your thought patterns and inner reactivity. Possibly, you've been accustomed to analyzing or dissecting your thoughts. You're not used to consciously experiencing what you're feeling. Experiencing thoughts on this level can feel all encompassing, especially if you don't like how you feel about them. If you find yourself either trying to change a thought or believing it holds the deepest truth to who you are, then you're lost to your thoughts.

What would it feel like, then, if you considered each thought to be merely content *moving through* your brain? Instead of analyzing or changing the thought, notice how it affects your relationship to your physical body. For instance, can you feel your physical body as you read this sentence? Are you able to be specific about what sensations you feel? What's your degree of comfort with this exploration? How long can you stay with feeling them before you go unconscious? As you're able to be completely honest with yourself about what you experience inside, you'll move in a direction that allows you to create the conditions for natural healing to take place. If you can't be completely honest with yourself, you'll further your *unconscious* relationship with yourself.

When you're unable to remain consciously engaged with your inner experience, you automatically slip into an unconscious, adaptive mode of functioning. This *can* be a healthy response; it protects you until you can cultivate the self-awareness necessary to remain conscious of what you feel. If you're like most individuals, though, you aren't even aware that this happens, so you remain in the clutches of your own self-imposed limitations. Once you can be completely honest about your full experience *exactly as it is,* you've taken an important step toward true healing and awakening. You'll be less likely to remain unconscious about how you currently function.

Remember, you're not looking for a bottom line. You aren't trying to change anything or figure it out. You're simply noticing what you experience. With practice, you can learn to track when and how you go unconscious within yourself. While this may sound easy, the initial process can confuse or frustrate you if you aren't used to consciously experiencing yourself this way. If you become overwhelmed with this inner exploration, be easy with yourself. The simplest things are usually the most difficult to master.

Most clients I've worked with were surprised by how much of their energy was caught up in past experiences, leaving them incapable of consciously moving with the natural flow of life. *Being completely honest with yourself about what you think and feel, as well as how you behave—layer upon layer—is an effective way to deeply heal, evolve your consciousness and re-integrate the energy caught up in those past experiences.* I haven't found a better way to develop personal power than to become a master of your own experience. "To know thyself" is your greatest asset.

This chapter presents a few examples of how the process of honest inner exploration can play out. These are true cases, but I've changed the names and details to keep the people anonymous. (See Chapter 8 for more examples.)

A woman named Claire came to sit with me so I could guide her in her inner exploration. A highly educated woman in her forties, Claire was raising her four-year-old son by herself. Meanwhile, she was dating a very wealthy man who repeatedly rejected the option of marriage—a situation that left her feeling increasingly unwanted with every failed ultimatum. In addition, her boyfriend lived a very social existence, spending most evenings out. He wanted her to accompany him, but she felt guilty about not staying home with her son. She'd hoped that her boyfriend would eventually tire of his lifestyle, but she was losing hope that he'd ever settle down to become an appropriate father figure. She wanted to leave the relationship, but the prospect of being on her own frightened her. She couldn't find enough clarity within herself to determine the healthiest direction to take. As a result, she felt unhappy and conflicted.

Claire showed me very quickly how she functioned; it was obvious that she experienced tremendous self-judgment about the cycle of fear that trapped her. She was constantly looking for a way to go unconscious so she wouldn't have to feel it. Both choices—to stay in the relationship and leave her son alone every night or to leave the relationship and be alone—left her feeling conflicted and in the clutches of fear. Then, whenever she noticed she was caught up in fear, she unconsciously overrode the experience by detaching from the feeling. Since she couldn't successfully leave her boyfriend or persuade him to marry her, she concluded that *she* was weak. This became her self-imposed identity.

I knew she'd have to cultivate the ability to consciously feel and observe her inner dynamic without trying to change her experience. The story of her "being weak" was a polarized expression of the myriad reactions and conditioned thought patterns held within her bodymind. This configuration was her adaptation. Therefore, the internal conflict was not the problem; it was merely the way she tolerated being alive with her conditioning in place.

So my primary goal was not to change her configuration or the story. Instead, I'd assist her as she developed a conscious relationship with the current expression of her story—on all levels of being. This internal conflict was full of useful information about how she unconsciously functioned from her *core belief*, but she'd never see or feel it unless she could access it consciously. She needed to open to it little by little, to learn what she needed to learn, while "accommodating" a new pattern of energetic flow, on all levels of her being. As all that bound energy self-corrected, it had to go somewhere in her system, so she'd need to integrate the new flow of raw energy. Simultaneously, she'd have to cultivate her developing awareness throughout her physiology.

In our work together, we needed to track how engaged she could remain with her current experience without re-traumatizing herself. She needed to learn how to diminish the intense charge that coursed through her system and knocked her unconscious. Little by little, she noticed when and how she went unconscious. She also witnessed the conclusions she came to about herself whenever she felt her inner conflict. She had to learn for herself that she identified with her thoughts and reactions. She explored what the inner conflict of fear and weakness *felt* like in her physical body—feeling the actual physical sensations. Where were the blocks and holdings in her energetic configuration? How did this inner conflict show up in her daily life? How did it affect her? Who or what within, wanted to be compassionately seen, felt and validated? Asking these questions directed her inner exploration, at least initially.

One day, in the middle of a session, she asked me what I thought about her relationship problems. She realized she was trying to change her boyfriend into the person she wanted him to be, so *she* wouldn't have to experience feelings of terror if he chose to leave her because she couldn't be who he wanted her to be.

I told her that it was a good insight; complete honesty was one of the most important tools in the process of self-exploration. She looked bewildered as I spoke and then interrupted to ask what I meant by *complete honesty*. I replied that it took tremendous courage to look within herself to discover her genuine feelings and to examine the true motivations behind her behaviors. It was only through this process that she could move into a more conscious understanding of her relationship with herself, which would lead to a more conscious understanding of her relationship with others.

I explained that she most likely wasn't able to move on with her life because undeveloped aspects within her were caught in an *ongoing* expression of fear. Every time she tried to be on her own, she experienced the earlier mappings of her conditioning getting enlivened. In essence, past experiences of fear were holding her captive, but at the same time, the existence of those aspects was the very reason she could still function in the world. They held an intense charge so *she wouldn't have to feel it directly*.

I told her that she had to learn how to meet the needs of those inner aspects. They felt overwhelmed. The girl is always mother to the woman, therefore she had to *re-parent* herself by acknowledging and validating for herself what she currently experienced. In turn, this would provide care for the younger, undeveloped aspects within her conscious awareness. She couldn't mature if these aspects remained isolated from her and stuck in past experiences. She also needed the time and practice to remain engaged with her experiences in an honest way *while consciously being with and feeling into the physical expressions of the fear* she felt.

As her relationship to herself becomes fuller and healthier, the stuck expressions will organically move toward completion. Then she'll be able to understand and directly experience an awakening—that while these experiences and feelings are happening within her, they don't define her. Ultimately, she'll no longer remain as identified with her thoughts or her inner reactivity, and *that's* the goal: to consciously move through the past and be delivered into the ever-present moment. Her ability to be honest with herself while on this journey will constantly deliver her into a new relationship with what's real and true *for her*.

As *you* move deeper within yourself, you'll encounter different levels of stunted development that you'll want to consciously move through. You'll use different tools at different stages. This work is a continual process that encompasses all the levels of your being. First, however, you must learn the fundamentals. Having this foundation—which includes the tools and insights that teach you how to safely move into and remain engaged with your experiences—will give you the potential to successfully navigate your own inner journey.

Complete Honesty at Work

Here's a different perspective to consider. It explains how complete honesty works.

If you're like most people, you aren't conscious of your relationship with the victim/perpetrator cycle. Depending on your conditioning, most of you play either an active role or a passive role in your relationships. It's one of the ways you interface with the world. If you see yourself as the passive one, you feel more comfortable in the victim role, while you see your adversary as playing the perpetrator. If you play the more active role in your relationship dynamic, you feel more comfortable with the role of the perpetrator, while viewing your adversary as the victim.

Both parties have very strong feelings about the roles they play and the role their adversary plays. In this duality, we convince ourselves that our position, whatever it is, is right, so we have to make the other person wrong. We'll fight with all our might to persuade the other person to submit to our will.

Society looks much more kindly on the victim role because it's the more socially acceptable behavior. Most of us identify with the guiltless victim. We don't believe perpetrators are *normal*. But here's an enlightening quote: "Behind every victim is a perpetrator and behind every perpetrator is a victim." We can't acknowledge to ourselves that we play the opposite role in moments, let alone have the awareness needed to explore how we do it. This would take tremendous honesty. We'd have to be able to stay conscious as we explored our inner motivation. So victims remain oblivious to their own acts as the perpetrator and vice versa.

Yet we all do it all the time, in a myriad of ways that don't have anything to do with physical harm. We just can't see it; we're conditioned to see only the obvious and what's more comfortable.

The reason for this is simple, yet ingenious: since we genuinely *think* we *are* our thoughts, beliefs, and reactions, we go unconscious or turn off our awareness whenever our intense inner charge overwhelms us—when we experience those "intolerable" physical sensations that correspond to emotions, such as shame, vulnerability, self-hatred, etc.— even if it's just for a second. We have an unconscious relationship with ourselves that filters out whatever doesn't fit our identified self-image. If our motivation is to feel good about ourselves and look good to others, we're unable to accept that we could possibly have acted as a perpetrator.

You see how the mind works? If you're lost to your own conditioning, your ability to be truly honest about your motivations is limited. You convince yourself that you didn't really behave that way, or you find a way to intellectually justify your behavior. The alternative is just too intense. Your behavior, therefore, ceases to be true, at least to you. Waking up to your relationship in this dynamic takes sincerity and tremendous self- compassion, as well as an ability to remain consciously engaged with how you function—meaning your internal motivations, your internal conflicts, and your external behaviors.

In order to develop a fuller relationship with yourself, you must include the whole picture (that is, all sides of a situation) in your inner exploration as honestly as you can, layer upon layer. This can be a daunting task for anyone since it takes time and practice to be able to do this work with complete honesty. It's important to note here that as you move deeper inside yourself, you'll find layers of truthfulness as you experience yourself and your inner motivations with more clarity. In other words, *what may seem true on the surface may not be when you dig deep.*

As you learn more about how you function, your first response may be to try to stop the behavior that generates those intolerable feelings. Over time, though, you'll discover that every person on the planet does some dance around the inner distortions they carry. You'll also learn to consciously use relationships responsibly.

As I said earlier, the key to effective inner exploration is to be completely honest with yourself about how you currently function, moment-to-moment, while remaining engaged with the physical expression of your experience. Therefore, you learn to consciously experience what you physically feel (the blocks, holdings, and sensations), question your inner motivations (the deepest truth of your actions), and discover how and when you go unconscious. Important questions drive your inner exploration. Your self-judgment about yourself and the inner distortions that you function from eventually soften as you're able to feel compassion for your own suffering. Simultaneously, you'll consciously feel healing, re-calibration and integration taking place within you.

The Transmutation of Suffering

When you resist reality as it is, you suffer. You go unconscious because you aren't internally resourced enough to accommodate the fullness of your experience. Most likely, you'll need to be properly supported as you move inward and wake up within the story that's being held in time. Gaining conscious momentum allows you to re-establish clarity.

I suggested to Claire that developing inner clarity right away might be too overwhelming, since she'd gone unconscious by detaching from her physical sensations and becoming identified with the stories some time ago. Those stories have established a type of momentum. This is not a small "issue" to overcome or fix. *This* was her current energetic configuration and the ongoing expression of her core belief; *it* would determine her experience. The stories and her relationship to them would potentially lead her back into her innate wholeness. Also, *she* herself gave the aspects their roles to play so she could function more comfortably within herself. This process would bring her back into a conscious relationship with those lost aspects and allow her to reclaim and integrate them back into the whole. Annihilating the aspects wouldn't work since they're doing their job to keep her intact and functioning, at least from the perspective of her beliefs.

For now, I told her, it would be enough to validate for herself that she felt stuck. Together, we'd begin the process of exploring that stuck place *inside* so *she* could wake up to how she currently functioned and meet the needs of each aspect within her. She needed not only to remain consciously engaged with what was being held within the stuck experience, but also to allow the new way she'd experience herself to emerge, little by little.

Initially, Claire wanted to get rid of the stuck experience; therefore, she kept trying to overcome or override it. I suggested instead that there might be information for her within the experience of *stuckness* that could help her develop. By diminishing the intensity of her experience, she could be with it consciously and learn what she needed to learn. To develop more self-awareness, however, she might need to be properly supported if she couldn't remain conscious through the entire experience. She'd have to move through layers of her own self-judgment while experiencing the release of old blocks and holdings, as well as accommodate a new energetic flow that would move through areas that had previously been blocked. Furthermore, *awareness* would be waking up to the ongoing identification with her beliefs and thought patterns currently held within the bodymind.

Claire looked at me as though I just asked her to walk over hot coals in her bare feet. I reminded her that her relationship to herself was and would always be the most important relationship she'd ever have. It served as a template for all her other relationships. If she didn't know how to honestly explore her own inner dynamics, if she couldn't learn to validate and nurture her own undeveloped aspects, how could she expect to have an intimate relationship with another person?

Initially, I looked for an indirect way for her to become aware of and feel her inner charge. Over time, she was able to work more directly as she built up the capacity to remain conscious and accommodate what she felt. I then taught her how to use her physical body as a way to engage her inner dynamics. She explored how the stuck spot felt in her physical body and tracked her corresponding energy flow. Together, we explored how she lived her day-to-day life: trying to protect herself from feeling the multitude of reactions to the stories that she functioned from, within her conditioned bodymind. This exploration became part of how we engaged that inner dynamic she felt as "the stuck place."

It would have been easy to tell her to leave her boyfriend, but I knew that wasn't going to consciously bring *her* up against her inner dynamic so it could self-correct from the inside first. From my perspective, she needed to be able to accommodate the inner fluctuations and intensity that came with being totally honest about her experience and her deepest motivations. She needed to become more *self-referred* so she could rest into herself naturally.

Here's what I mean: when we don't complete all the stages of development during childhood, the personality, bodymind, and ego can't develop properly. In this case, we can become *other-referred,* meaning we remain outwardly focused and dependent, looking for a constant signal from someone outside ourselves that we're safe, just as we did in infancy. This becomes the infant's survival strategy. Human beings are biologically wired to survive, so when we feel threatened, even as infants, we look for ways to come back to homeostasis. If this inner dynamic remains intact and unresolved from its point of origin, we'll continue to unconsciously function from it. We certainly can't be authentically relational when we're chronically outwardly focused. When we're *self-referred,* on the other hand, we remain in constant connection with our ongoing honest experience on all levels of being. We experience ourselves as autonomous emotional and physical beings, which is ultimately a more comfortable and fuller inner experience.

I explained to Claire that we all avoid things that make us feel uncomfortable until we can experience them with less intensity and more clarity. Of course, many of us override our discomfort so we can feel artificially empowered: "Look at me. I'm taking charge of my life! I am determining my destiny!" We create personas in order to have a favorable, preconceived result. While this way of functioning works for a period of time, eventually our personas won't hold up any longer, and we feel the breakdown of the artificial "self" we constructed. For some of us, this might appear to happen in an instant. For others, it might appear more gradually. However it happens, it's rarely a comfortable experience.

The notion of consciously *opening and moving into and through* your experience, as opposed to *overcoming* it, is not very popular in our culture. We want to get rid of anything we perceive as unattractive or messy. Most people don't visit a therapist's office to move into their experience so they can get to know it better. They go hoping to be relieved of the distress they're currently experiencing. And there is a wide variety of facilitators to choose from who make "overcoming" your experience sound very attractive. So it can feel daunting, even unnerving, the first time I suggest to clients the possibility of exploring their experiences from the inside, just as they are.

Here's another example. If a client told me she didn't want to be overweight any longer, I'd explain that there was a valid reason for her extra weight. If she really wanted to shed it, she first had to *feel* the weight on her body and come to understand what it did for her. As she developed more self-awareness, the weight would come off naturally while she learned to consciously feel and accommodate the experience from which the weight protected her. In essence, the weight helped her manage an intense feeling within herself.

Not wanting to feel her current experience of the extra weight exposes a resistance to acknowledging reality as it currently is. She has to work with her *full experience,* which includes both "wanting to lose weight" *and* "being with and feeling the extra weight on her physical body." Tracking both experiences inside herself—and really acknowledging how they both feel—can bring to light subconscious information about herself. Then, as her weight comes off, she'll have to consciously feel a continuum of experiences as she transitions into a new ongoing relationship with herself. She'll also have to consciously accommodate her experience of feeling physically lighter.

She can't skip these steps if she wants to experience a deeper connection with herself. If she tries to *get rid of* the weight before she moves into a more conscious and deeper understanding of her relationship to it, she won't be functioning within the healing window. Therefore, integration—the path to deep and true healing and, in this case, lasting weight loss—won't take place. That's why diets don't work for everyone.

In today's world, there's a lot at stake if you can appear like you've got your act together. Lose that, and you could lose your friends, your job, your social status, your parent's approval, even your way of life. For many of us, this prospect is terrifying, so if you're like most people, you do everything in your power to keep that façade going, even if it's only a façade.

I have great empathy and respect for people who have the wherewithal to move into a more honest relationship with themselves. As I've said throughout this book, however, there's an art to going inside and exploring your inner terrain, so begin your journey wisely. The deeper the grooves, the more astute you need to be when moving inward. You don't yet know what you'll set in motion once you have some momentum under your belt. Even though the fundamentals—such as consciously working with your current experience as it is and employing complete honesty —are the same, your unique fears and strengths must be considered. *Remember, this work is not about re-traumatizing yourself.*

When you enter the "inner world," it's vital that you learn to acknowledge your current experience with judicious consideration and beneficial intent. Ultimately, only *you* can feel how to proceed. Your psychotherapist, bodymind facilitator, spiritual teacher, or whomever you enlist to help, therefore, *must* have personal experience with the process. If they aren't effective at helping you awaken, by assisting you as you consciously work with your unique patterns of conditioning, by feeling and engaging their current expression on all levels of being, then keep searching for someone who can. (See Chapter 10 for more insight into choosing a facilitator.)

The "Quick Fix"

We live in a time where we can "seemingly" acquire whatever we desire in the instant it takes us to click a button. We purchase a product online, charge it on a credit card, and instantly we feel a sense of power and satisfaction . . . or so we think. However, what we may have unconsciously experienced is the discharge of our rising energy that was causing us to feel mentally and emotionally frightened and unclear. For a window of time, we feel more comfortable inside ourselves, until the charge builds again. Yet our current energetic configuration and the belief we're currently living will perpetuate the same patterns over and over until they're consciously met. In the long run, the quick fix notion creates nothing but pain and disappointment.

You have to do the work if you're interested in developing a healthier, more integrated experience of yourself. (I use the term *healthy* interchangeably with the word *natural* to show that natural, true health is the opposite of a preconceived notion of health.) A quick fix only restores the personas you've become accustomed to, the identified version of yourself that's been conditioned since early childhood to think and react a certain way. To live authentically takes time, just as it does to get to know a new friend or a potential partner on a first date. It takes time and practice to understand how you function. It's not easy to awaken to how much of your energy is captured in the past.

It makes sense to inquire about your past experiences as a way to begin the process of developing a healthier, more integrated experience of your true nature. Who and what you think you are is a direct result of all your life experiences, past and present. Much of your deepest conditioning, however, is expressed and caught in early childhood experiences. The myriad ways you identify yourself based on something that happened in your past is a dance you must approach with respect. You didn't fall into this illusion overnight, so you need time to appreciate its complexities and to work through the theme and patterns that are intricately interconnected with all the levels of your being.

Think of the journey toward self-awareness this way: if you were driving from Florida to California but somehow lost your way, you might call someone for directions. Before anyone could help you, though, you'd first have to explain where you were. If you didn't know exactly (because you were really lost), you could still give helpful hints: "It's cold outside," or "The area code is 401." You'd have to accurately describe the outer terrain in order for the person to discover where you were and help guide you back in the direction toward California.

There's no way to skip all the states you need to travel through on your way. After all, if you drove through those states, each one would hold different associations for you. The way you experienced yourself in each state—and how you related to the people you encountered—would provide information about how you currently functioned, as well as providing memories of your journey. If you were able to be honest with yourself about what you felt, if you took the time to reflect on your inner experiences without grasping onto them, you'd be in a very different place within yourself by the time you actually arrived in California.

Taking the journey consciously brings about a fuller, deeper, more intimate relationship with yourself. In the end, you can look back with perspective to observe that each state brought with it a unique way of experiencing yourself, whether you realized it at the time or not. You can't skip over these experiences or pretend that you had them artificially. *You have to experience them directly for yourself.* Yet your experiences don't define you.

The Bodymind Relationship

Since we're all co-creators of our lives, our lives mirror back to us who and what we believe we are. Therefore, observing our relationship to ourselves and others can be very enlightening, especially when the exploration is done through taking complete responsibility for our inner experience. Just becoming aware that we're out of balance begins to shift us into a healthier relationship with ourselves, as well as with our lives.

Attaining a healthy relationship with your bodymind is a process, like peeling the layers of an onion. Each layer reveals a different flavor of the story that's looking for "its" resolution. Each layer finds its validity through your ability to feel compassion for its unique story. By not skipping steps, you create a natural movement that creates new pathways that are a byproduct of you directly experiencing reality as it is. Remember: *If you're used to being out of balance, that state becomes your accepted way of functioning. But it's not your truest expression, and it's not who and what you are.*

Feeling and emotions are not indicators of who and what we are. Yet it's a fact that we feel exactly what we feel, moment-to-moment. When we experience our thoughts and emotions while disconnected from physical sensation, however, it's very easy to collapse into and identify with our inner dynamic. Therefore, we have to start where we are, which is usually a place that we don't like and have been resisting.

In reality, you always experience the opposite of where you are in your process. Let me explain. At the start of the process, you're unconscious of—and disengaged from—your experience. The further along you get, the more directly and clearly you feel your distortions. This can feel intense, yet you're actually more aware and integrated. You feel your experience more intimately at this point because you *can*. You no longer need a buffer between you and the distortions you carry. If the earlier layers have been sufficiently supported and engaged, your work has produced an integration delivering you into a new relationship with the whole of yourself. You now experience yourself differently. As you become more self-aware, you're *more* able to consciously open to and *feel* your current, moment-to-moment experience of yourself. You're more and more able, therefore, to move consciously through life. The more momentum you gain, the more directly engaged you become with your distortions and the more aligned you become with your natural rhythms.

That's why humility is so important in this work. When you've spent enough time with the process to become more accustomed to being with your experience exactly as it is, you recognize that there may always be another layer of the onion or a deeper mode of function where you're still lost to distortion or identity. I've seen "enlightened masters" act as though they're beyond this scenario, but it can trap *anyone*. As you become more awake and integrated, your distortions become even more hidden and well defended, so being able to feel and track the subtleties becomes even more vital to your success. It really does take tremendous sincerity and honesty, as well as practice, to sit in silence and feel the subtleties within as you do your exploration. Since we can't always see our own blind spots, we at times need assistance from someone who has experience with the process.

Every layer of the onion brings about a different mode of function. As you work your way through them, you'll need the proper support to feel comfortable enough to directly experience each new stage of your development. For example, as you discover a more direct relationship to *feeling,* you might feel aches and pains in the physical body more consciously, while simultaneously experiencing places in the psyche that feel stuck and therefore angry and frightened.

These holdings in the bodymind are there to remind you that not only have you clenched, but you're also simultaneously identified with "something" other than your true essence. This is information for you, as well as a pointer to where to bring your awareness. This experience is an entryway into a deeper relationship with yourself. *This* is how you engage your inner dynamic. Since everything is interconnected, this shift in awareness affects all the other levels of your being as well.

Awakening is a deliberate, organic process. You take the next step because it becomes self-evident. You can feel it's your next stage. It's not forced. You know enough not to try to be somewhere before you're authentically there. As you move through the process, you'll develop your own inner parent, and as you mature further, you'll develop the *teacher within*. Through this process, you'll cultivate wisdom.

The Individuation Process

Even people with the best of childhoods still have to individuate from their parents or caregivers to become autonomous enough to comfortably think and feel for themselves. Ideally, parents, teachers, and therapists help you individuate since individuation on any level is challenging. Everyone experiences a charge around self-reliance. Didn't you feel thrilled the first time you stood in your own space and could feel for yourself whether to turn left or turn right? It's part of human evolution.

Infancy imprints a powerful charge onto the infant bodymind—all that dependency and the driving need to attach, for example. It takes courage, as well as sufficient internal and external resources, to feel those charges consciously as an adult. Most people aren't aware that so much of their inner discomfort comes from early childhood. The infant experience can be brutal; everyone has to go through it and no one makes it through unscathed. When an infant experiences trauma, such as "an absence of care," a tremendous charge immediately builds, leaving a lasting imprint on the whole system. The more trauma a person endured during infancy, the bigger the imprint on the whole system.

Most people detach themselves from those charges in order to survive, so they can continue to function. As a result, they don't understand that those charges are often exactly the places where they're stuck in their development. These strong inner charges map onto the other developmental stages throughout the physiology, hence the need to work with the body.

There is no substitute for directly and consciously engaging all facets of your being. You can't transcend your distortions exclusively if you want to live a conscious existence. In other words, waking up as pure consciousness does not make all your distorted ways of functioning magically go away. Eventually, as you come back from your transcending practice, your current experience of yourself, as you are, awaits you.

The process is different for everyone. In fact, for some individuals, the process doesn't get rough until after they've had their first awakening experience. Ideally, you'd adequately develop the ego and personality as you awaken so you can comfortably experience the transcendental nature of your being. (Remember, since you *are* pure consciousness, you don't have to develop it. You only need to discover what lies in the way, preventing you from directly experiencing what you already are.) If you have unfinished business from early childhood expressing itself through the structures of your ego personality, it will hinder your ability to experience your true nature on all levels of your being in a seamlessly integrated manner. While it's possible for you to have a direct experience of pure consciousness before you've moved through the developmental stages of individuation and autonomy, you cannot fully and deeply awaken until you've seamlessly integrated *all* the levels of your being.

Being with Our Experience as It Is

I once worked with a 60-something-year-old woman named Natalie who experienced a lot of day-to-day fear. When she wasn't feeling overwhelmed, she was as sharp as a tack. But her brain was so overstimulated that it felt like a light bulb that wouldn't shut off and ultimately created many sleepless nights. Whenever she left the house, the expressions of her core belief became so enlivened that her mind scattered. She sometimes forgot where she was, which caused her to panic. The prospect of getting lost—along with the attendant fears of being hurt or taken advantage of—furthered her anxieties. As a way to diminish the intensity of her experience, she refused to leave her house alone.

This adaptive mode of functioning created some comfort for her since she wasn't constantly pushing herself beyond her capacity to remain consciously engaged with her experience. Yet as her charge built up again, she'd redecorate her home by moving her furniture around. From her perspective, she wanted to feel that some sort of change was taking place in her life and that she was accomplishing something. In reality, the intensity of her inner experience drove her to look for a much needed unconscious discharge. She organized every aspect of her life to detach from her internal experience of the belief and to discharge the rising energy she experienced as anxiety. This is how she kept herself safe from consciously experiencing whatever it was that felt too intense.

I could see that her methods had worked for her, but only up to a point. She had created her adaptations, and they did what she wanted them to do. Deep down, Natalie knew she couldn't find what she was genuinely looking for by experiencing herself through this very limited internal configuration. While it kept her safe from inner experiences that felt too intense, it stopped her from living a fulfilling life.

Most individuals —consciously as well as subconsciously—choose to limit their experience of themselves so they won't feel the very intense inner charges they carry. The separation keeps them safe from feeling whatever experience they can't safely and comfortably accommodate, especially when there is past trauma involved. In reality, they override their current experience of themselves (that is, go unconscious about what they're really feeling) so they can believe they're making progress while the deeper distortion remains intact. Ultimately, this becomes a self-defining and self-limiting approach. Until they are sufficiently resourced and have the capacity to experience themselves directly, many people prefer a shortcut to the natural and organic integration of their whole being. *It's not until they have a conscious relationship with how they override their current experiences—and what that feels like within themselves—that they want to be with what's authentic and real.*

Natalie had been programmed in her previous therapy to *override* her current experience, which was deemed not only unhealthy, but the culprit of her unhappiness. When I sit with individuals, I meet them where *they* are and work with them to have a more conscious experience of how they function in the moment, so I knew better than to label her. Instead, I wanted to support her as she was, so she could experience her inner dynamic with sufficient clarity to develop more self-awareness. This type of support would allow her to experience herself directly and see her past in a different light. It would help her develop continuity mentally, emotionally, and physically in seamless ways that weren't possible before.

Natalie was a very creative and energetic woman with a multitude of talents, so her inability to experience a fuller relationship with herself left her feeling deeply dissatisfied. When describing her life, she'd say she was so bored she could scream. Her previous psychotherapist tried to help her find a social activity she enjoyed (such as joining a club) so she could meet other people her age. No matter how many suggestions her therapist gave her, however, Natalie couldn't follow through on any of them. This made her think of and define herself as a failure, a lost cause, all because she couldn't move past or overcome what she *wasn't* feeling to do the simple things her therapist asked her to do.

One day, she called me in despair, crying that she didn't want to live anymore. I asked if I could help her diminish the intensity of her experience. When she acquiesced, I asked her to take a seat and sit straight up with her back away from the back of the chair and press her feet gently into the floor. Once she relaxed a little, she complained that her life wasn't working for her anymore. In her confusion, she didn't know what to do or where to turn.

She began the process of reconnecting with herself as she moved inward, feeling her physical body a little bit at a time. While she kept her legs engaged by lightly pressing her feet into the ground, I asked her to touch her right shoulder with her left hand and move it in a circle around the shoulder and then down the arm, touching and moving the skin back and forth every half inch or so until she reached her fingers. Then I asked her to repeat the exercise on the opposite shoulder and arm. Then I asked her to take her right hand and put in on her left shoulder and simultaneously put her left hand on her right shoulder, crisscrossing them, and move them downward across her chest. I then asked her to gently touch both legs, starting at her hips and then moving down about a half inch at a time until she got to her knees. As she finished, I asked her if she felt any pressure in her head. She replied that she felt pressure in her forehead. I asked her to grab a handful of hair at the top of her head and pull it up from her scalp while moving it in a slow clockwise circle, feeling the sensation as she did.

Afterward, she said she felt calmer. I told her she was no longer escalating her inner distortions; she'd just smoothed out the rapid rising energy that was distorting her emotional experience of herself. In essence, this is what parents do for a crying child. The physical contact children receive when parents pick them up taps off the inner charge that had created a sense of discomfort. Children can only handle so much current moving through them before their discomfort level becomes too great. If they're asked to handle more than they can comfortably accommodate, they'll split off or disassociate as a way to handle the overwhelming experience.

When you're experiencing great distress, it's not helpful to stay cooking in that intense inner charge. If you do, you'll spend most of your energy trying to defend against it. Meanwhile, the mental/emotional body becomes highly activated and distorted. Within this experience is valuable information you could use, if only you could become conscious of it, but you can't observe it objectively when you're caught in the mad rush of your own rising energy. If you can diffuse the charge, you can experience yourself in a less distorted manner, which is a much better time to begin your self-exploration.

Such was the case for Natalie. Now that she was calmer, she could hear what I had to say. I told her that from my perspective, her previous therapist had tried to get her to be two steps ahead of where she actually was. Natalie said she told her therapist honestly what she was going through. I responded that her therapist was so busy trying to change her experience so she'd *look* healthier, she missed the most obvious part of therapy: supporting her as she currently "is" so she could actually *become* healthier.

Natalie said her therapist had already explained to her that her childhood experiences had instilled fear and anxiety in her. The explanation made sense, and it helped her understand it. But now, as an adult, she felt as though she was supposed to be able to change her behavior. Yet she couldn't. Consequently, she felt like and identified herself as a failure.

Unfortunately, just having an intellectual understanding of your childhood—and the role it played in shaping you—is not enough to enable deep healing. It's a great beginning, but there are many stages thereafter that you must consciously engage, move through, and feel before you can truly heal.

I told Natalie that being a failure was the way she was used to thinking about herself. It was how she'd come to know herself, the identity she'd adopted as a young girl. But it wasn't who and what she really was. The fear and anxiety that resulted from her beliefs and conditionings clouded her ability to experience herself from a truer place. Not being able to rest into herself during her childhood did not—could not—imbue her with a sense of safety and security. She had so identified with the intensity of her thoughts and feelings that she accepted that they defined who and what she was. But, I assured her, she was mistaken.

She then asked me how she could stop doing it. I told her that she didn't have to stop. First and foremost, she'd wired herself internally to be this way, so she couldn't simply turn it off. It would be as foolish and destructive as asking a train barreling down the track to immediately reverse direction.

Since she hadn't found the support she needed to safely open to and feel her experiences as they were, she was caught in a cycle of trying to overcome or override those experiences. This pattern of resistance naturally resulted in feelings of exhaustion and deep despair. Once she believed she was a failure for not overcoming her issues, the cycle would begin again. The good news, I told her, was that she had enough inner wisdom and sense of self to be aware that something didn't feel right. Even when an authority figure had given her instructions, she was able to be honest enough with herself to feel that something was missing. This told me that she had the self-awareness to do the inner work and the ego-strength to be completely honest with herself.

She hadn't been able to move through her childhood developmental phases in a healthy, continuous manner, so she wasn't able to calmly rest into herself. As a result, she had projected her disowned fears and anxieties out onto the world, which explained why she now viewed the world as unsafe. I told her these experiences or stories were happening *within her*.

Deep Healing Happens Degrees at a Time

Surges of emotion can't be overridden. They can't be swept under the rug or zapped out of existence. At least not in a healthy way. Natalie's strong emotions stemmed from specific childhood stresses. They are imprints from certain past experiences that Natalie had come to think and believe was the true *her*. Because of her unconscious inner dynamic, she was reliving those experiences over and over. Any time they got activated, such as when she tried to leave the house, she felt the strong charge and reactions they held become enlivened, and she therefore collapsed into them. These strong reactions can feel very real and overwhelming, which can create an even more distorted experience of the self. I call this inner cycle "story chasing."

At this stage of her development, the healthiest way for Natalie to work with her inner dynamic was to compassionately care for the place inside that was having a reaction before, during, and after she imagined leaving the house. She had to learn to recognize what she was feeling and to realize that it was happening *within* her. In essence, she had to learn to care for herself while she experienced her inner reactions. She needed to accommodate this stage of development before she could consciously awaken to the conditioned responses that stemmed from her childhood experiences. But this behavior obviously hadn't been modeled for her in early childhood, so she simply did not have a reference for it.

I told her it was all right (and even expected) to feel daunted by a challenge that left her feeling as if she couldn't control anything. She'd slowly come to know herself in a different way, and little by little, she wouldn't feel so intimidated. When she could be completely honest with herself about what she experienced internally—as well as what motivated her behavior—she'd cultivate a different relationship within her physiology, one that allowed her to rest inward. As she became better able to be with her honest experience in the moment, she'd come to know, in a more direct way, that *she* wasn't the fear and anxiety she felt.

During our session, I asked her to explore her relationship to the emotions plaguing her. *Who or what within her was feeling fearful? What was its concern? Where was she experiencing this in her physical body? What did it feel like? What was the accompanying sensation? Was there clenching or an absence of flow?* As she felt more supported in her experience, she rested into herself without having to force an outcome.

This was not going to be a quick fix. To be successful, she'd have to continue to be with her honest experience as it was while also keeping herself in the present. I explained to her that true healing happened naturally, layers at a time. Eventually, she'd feel self-referred enough to be able to be with her experience without my external support. Unfortunately, she had several incomplete stages of early childhood development that had piggybacked onto each other, so developing the new wiring would most likely be a great challenge. This incomplete developmental phase kept her caught in a constant fight-or-flight survival mode, having to remain well defended from her own inner reactions. As she woke up, she'd begin to feel her direct experience of this inner dynamic consciously, which can be very confusing without proper support.

I had to keep her experience of her external reality in focus during her inner exploration so she wouldn't get caught up in her distorted thought patterns. Ultimately, she was in the driver's seat. *She* had to know how much was too much. This is a delicate process. She'd have to feel her way through the different layers at a pace that didn't force or overwhelm her.

I told her that having an intellectual understanding of how her childhood stress structured her reactions was a wonderful and very useful step, but it was just the beginning. She had to learn how to *feel* within herself. She had to learn the guidelines for safely taking the journey inward. She had much to learn. Even after cultivating a healthier relationship with her internal experience, she still had to allow that experience to self-normalize in a way that was authentic for her.

Eventually, she understood that she was attempting to discharge her ongoing internal charge and the uncomfortable way in which she experienced herself by controlling her external environment. This way of functioning, however, couldn't really change anything; it was only a coping mechanism. She needed to work with and engage her inner dynamics in order for her relationship with the outer world to eventually shift. It would take practice for her to learn how to be with her experience as it was. I therefore supported her decision to stay home while she learned to remain engaged with and comfortably accommodate what she was feeling in the moment. When she experienced herself as less distorted, she'd organically feel a natural impulse to move back out into the world a little at a time.

This example emphasizes everything I've written about healing. For Natalie, simply leaving the house wasn't a valid barometer for healing, especially if she had to force herself to do it *under duress*. She could fake it to appear healthier, but life would eventually reflect her beliefs back to her over and over again until she couldn't ignore them any longer. She followed that path previously. It didn't work and led her to me.

Much of the work ahead lay in her ability to re-integrate the energy caught in all the highly charged fragments within herself. Her inner experiences felt very real to her. And they were real. Her identification with the experience, however, had clouded her fuller experience of who and what she truly was. As she learned more about how she functioned and as she could accommodate fuller expressions of her true nature, she'd experience herself more clearly.

As much as we'd like to, we simply can't skip steps.

Since she'd also expressed a momentary desire to die, we explored this, too. I told her that something *within* her wanted to die, which was very different from *her* wanting to die. I told her that every experience has a lifespan—a beginning, middle, and end—so if something within her wanted to die, she didn't need to keep it caught under constant duress. This energy wasn't the totality of who she was. We spent some time communicating with the aspect within her that wanted to die. As she consciously felt compassion for the suffering that she and this formed aspect currently shared, it found its own resolution. She allowed it to communicate its experience on a feeling level, while at moments speaking from that place directly. As this thought form was consciously experienced and she learned what she needed to learn, it organically released from her system.

The Uniqueness of Being

Healing happens at a unique pace for each individual. Furthermore, the process looks different for everyone. You can't push yourself to heal more quickly. You can't force yourself to heal differently from the way you will. It just doesn't work that way. All you can do is create the proper conditions to allow healing to take place. By accepting your experience as it is—without forcing yourself to be something or someplace else—you create a window in which the potential for self-correction can take place.

For example, if I cut myself by accident, I clean the wound to reduce the chance of infection. Then I cover the cut with a clean bandage so it can heal. I don't have to tell it how to heal. It heals on its own. If nature has within it the ability to heal a cut, then why shouldn't it also have the ability to heal my distortions on every level of my being? After all, everything is interconnected.

We are all different. We must have respect for how each and every individual functions. We are, after all, unique products of our inner beliefs and life experiences.

The integration process too is unique to each of us. You are your own individual snowflake amongst many other snowflakes. There is beauty and perfection in that. What's healthy for one person isn't necessarily healthy for another. Instead of forcing yourself to fit someone else's *image* of health, rest into where you are in the moment and live honestly from that place.

So even if you resist being honest in your inner exploration, you can at least be honest about that. You just have to acknowledge where you are right now—whatever way you currently function. There isn't one way of functioning that is "the right way." Do not judge the way you function; use it as information. Reflect on it as you get to know your inner landscape.

Most people do some dance around their beliefs and conditionings. As you develop more compassion in yourself for your current experiences, you can relax into the moment and be more honest and open in your inner exploration. The more you naturally function from your honest, direct experience, the more your harsh self-criticism naturally softens. When you take responsibility for whatever you feel inside yourself, you become more aware when you're *not* functioning consciously. You recognize when you're coasting on your identities and delusions, when you aren't being true to your inner experiences.

When you get frustrated or lose yourself to fear and confusion (and it will happen), you might project those feelings onto others or onto the world. As you're more and more honest with yourself, as you learn to genuinely feel what you truly feel, and as you take responsibility for what you experience, you'll interact with others from a place of empathy because you'll now understand how challenging *it has been to navigate* your own inner experiences.

Subtleties are very important in the healing process. The

greater the degree of integration you experience, the more subtle the expression of your distortions. Without an ability to feel your way through the nuances of your inner experiences, you aren't going to be able to discern what makes sense and what doesn't.

Discernment is a vital personal development tool, and you absolutely must cultivate it. It'll help you navigate your inner experiences throughout your lifetime. It makes it possible for you to develop confidence in yourself and in your abilities. Without discernment, all you can do is to function from desperation, fear, and dependence on others. When you consciously know what you feel and where you feel it inside yourself—and when you understand your relationship to these feelings—you'll have one of the greatest assets any individual could embody. This is the subject of the next chapter.

CHAPTER 5

Opening to the Infinite Flow of Life

Your currently held beliefs not only *flavor* your internal and external life experiences, but actually *create* them. Here's an example: If you believe you aren't safe in the world, then you'll *have the experience* of not feeling safe in the world. It becomes the filter through which you see everything.

Life, as they say, is all perception. It follows then that your perception of life must resonate or align with your beliefs. One supports the other. So if five people experience the same event, all five may have a different perception of it because their beliefs color their reality.

Therefore, the question is: Do we see life *as it really is* or *as we think it is*? Many years ago, I heard a lecture in which the speaker said that spiritual enlightenment is nothing more than *seeing things as they actually are*. Enlightenment, in other words, is waking up from the dream of your mind and seeing things without the filters of your beliefs—through "new eyes," as the mystics said. I thought this was brilliant! So simply stated and so very true.

When you're lost to your conditioning and you truly

believe that you are your thoughts, ideas, associations, and reactions, it's not so simple to directly feel the truth of that statement within yourself. Moreover, if you had any type of trauma in early childhood, you've been conditioned to experience yourself through your psycho-physiological distortions. This distorted identification, held within the bodymind, becomes your reality. While this is obviously not the ultimate truth of your existence, it absolutely is what you experience.

In order for you to see things as they actually are, you have to learn to consciously *see* and *feel* what's currently in front of you in this moment, exactly as it is. You become conscious of your inner landscape when you can remain engaged with the subtleties of its expression on all levels of being. You're not grasping at or pushing away your experiences. You're effortlessly flowing with the movement of life. You experience *true freedom* when you're completely open to the infinite flow of life, in this and every instant.

How We Distort Our Natural Flow

Your reactions to external events and encounters come from your relationship to your inner landscape. When you cannot consciously and openly feel your current experience all the way through from beginning to end, you create a distortion of your life force—your energetic flow—that you may also experience as an inner charge. You experience this charge as an intensity that's too much to deal with directly. The greater the charge, the more your "survival tactics" automatically kick in. So to survive, you disconnect from the experience in that moment to dampen its impact enough to make it more tolerable.

This sounds antithetical to true health, but functioning

this way protects you when a charge is too great for you to remain in touch with it. The danger of "losing it" can feel like a real threat if you're forced to stay with an experience that's too intense. The body has wisdom, though, and it knows how much is too much. In the same way, you wouldn't send too much electrical current through a wire not suited to carry that much voltage.

To keep from being overloaded, you dampen the experience as a way to remain functional, sane, and possibly even alive. Now that your inner experience is distorted, however, it consequently frightens you. You sense that it was too much for you to handle, which highlights a weakness—a feeling of fragility that tells you there's a disconnect within the system. In this reactive state, you believe your thoughts and reactions (for example, the fragility), and so you become *identified* with this distorted experience. You think it defines you, so you begin to think it is who and what you are. This becomes your ongoing, self-limiting inner dynamic.

Psychological and Spiritual Healing: Moving from Polarized Expressions Toward Integration

When an initial experience is too uncomfortable to be with consciously, we separate from it. If it feels very intense, we may even disassociate and/or fragment in relation to it. To adapt to our new unnatural state, we *polarize* the resulting inner distortion as a survival tactic and as a way to make it more comfortable to tolerate. The intensity held within the polarity depends on a number of factors, including your relationship to your conditioning and the degree to which you've become identified with it.

For example, let's say you're functioning from a core belief that states it's not safe to be on the planet—that your mental, emotional, and physical existence is in constant jeopardy. Now any time that you're engaged in the present moment, you'll feel more alive . . . and then immediately begin to feel unsafe. Since it's your core belief that you're not safe, part of you experiences that fear all the time, even if you aren't consciously aware of it. You develop associations with past memories of feeling unsafe and then think those experiences are the issues you have to overcome. You aren't consciously aware of your core belief since you've disconnected from deep feeling. Yet much of your focus in life is on trying to be safe. However, you can never experience the feeling of safety because you perceive yourself through the original belief that states that you are not safe. *Trying* to be safe, while not being able to *actually experience* safety, is a reaction and consequently becomes your inner bind. If pushed beyond what you can experience consciously (such as being present), the charged energy (such as fear) can become polarized to further diminish the strong reactions that are enlivened.

This is how it works: We shunt from one side of the polarization to the other as a way to regulate our overstimulation. When an experience begins to feel too overwhelming, we shunt to the non-feeling side. This makes it feel like a change, which is the point. We assume we've found a way out the other side, but we haven't escaped at all. Sooner or later feelings are enlivened in the non-feeling side and we shunt back again. All we've done is moved from one side to the other. The greater the charge, the quicker we shunt from side to side.

Any time we come up against an experience that challenges our core belief, we're automatically thrust into our polarized adaptation to keep the charge from feeling too overwhelming. If we experience one end of the polarization for too long, we unconsciously shunt to the opposite end. This gives our system a break from the intensity, but the price for this relief is that we have to continually reconfigure our energy patterns to keep ourselves from feeling.

Since this technique works, at least temporarily, it becomes our new way of functioning. Eventually, we become so used to operating this way that it feels like who and what we are, even though part of us knows it's not. Neither side of the polarization defines us. Both are distortions.

The undistorted experience—our true potential—lies in the *integration* of both sides. This understanding is especially relevant for those who want to spiritually awaken, live a consciously embodied existence, and/or recover from psychological imbalances or trauma.

As your integration takes place, you consciously experience your relationship to your conditioning—your beliefs, thought patterns, ideas, identities, and associations—in whatever form and on whatever level of your being they currently present themselves. As your relationship to your conditioning becomes more conscious, which means that you aren't grasping onto or avoiding any part of your inner experience, your distortions have the potential to organically release from your system. For this to happen, though, you must remain engaged with your current experience while being completely truthful with yourself about what you feel. You can't use "theory" as a means to intellectually understand your experience in order to avoid feeling uncomfortable. You absolutely have to see and directly feel for yourself what this split is doing for you. If you think you can skip this step because many spiritual, psychology and self-help books theorize why you have the experiences you have, you're wrong. Without honestly and consciously feeling your experience exactly as it is within the mental, emotional, and physical levels of your being, your psychological and spiritual healing will remain incomplete.

Sometimes, this may mean having to organically track your experience back to its original source. The process works this way: As you track what you feel, moving inward through the layers of your experience, you discover what you originally felt, as well as the conclusions you reached. This time, though, you remain conscious—as opposed to going unconscious—while in the experience. So when you experience a polarization of your energy, you aren't lost to your reaction, but instead, you're able to track your experience of both sides while observing and feeling your relationship to each. By doing this, neither side can remain in denial of the other. By validating the experience of each side, you reduce the tremendous inner charge. What once felt like "black or white" becomes gray. What once felt like "this or that" gradually moves toward "this *and* that." You're integrating both sides within the context of the whole.

This process takes time to integrate into your daily life. Most people don't usually have a conscious relationship with how they function relative to the many selves being expressed as polarizations, fragmentations, inner charges, reactions, binds, and identifications. They've blocked themselves off from their actual experience and walled off their reactions to the point that they really have no clue that anything, let alone a fuller experience of themselves, lies deep within their physical, mental, and emotional experience of themselves. Yet life always points them toward the way that helps them see things as they actually are.

Your polarized energy is an expression of your unconscious relationship to your belief. If it's doing its job, you won't even realize that you're currently wired this way. Yet inside, you're enduring the experience all the time.

Our suffering is the means by which we awaken and heal. Consciously *feeling our own distress* wakes us up to how we currently function to a greater degree. Then our conditioning doesn't have quite the same hold on us, which leaves us with an increasingly clearer perspective. In Eastern spiritual traditions, this is called the "wheel of karma." These karmic impressions are the deeply instilled grooves that are expressed through the bodymind.

For example, imagine walking around with a pebble in your shoe. If you don't feel and validate your own discomfort, you may keep walking. Unconsciously, you condition yourself into thinking that "this experience" is what walking feels like, as opposed to the reality that you're walking with a pebble in your shoe. *It's your ability to feel your own distress* (that is, your ability to notice that you have a pebble in your shoe) that wakes you up. How does this example apply to *your* life?

Resisting Our Current Experience

We're all clever people; we use food, exercise, alcohol, drugs, sex, meditation, spiritual seeking, overworking, shopping, constant traveling, socializing, or other compulsive activities as an adaptation to keep ourselves from the direct experience of our beliefs. We use these behaviors to keep ourselves from the internal experiences that feel overwhelming and disorienting. We're trying to avoid experiencing what we have repeatedly known. We're not just afraid of the unknown; we're also afraid of the known, which is why we chronically intellectualize our experiences.

To effectively engage the known, we must resource ourselves differently in relation to what we experience in the moment. Only then will our experience of ourselves change relative to our beliefs. This happens by being honest about our experience, as well as by gaining the ability to track how and when we go unconscious. We must cultivate a direct awareness of what our behaviors are doing for us. *We have to physically feel our experience.*

Very intense reactions can overshadow the direct experience of your essential Self and cause you to feel alone, divided, and frightened, especially when you're dealing with psychological fear. When you're caught in the clutches of this inner intensity, it feels very real. Since it becomes your primary experience, you convince yourself that it's who and what you are. If someone tries to tell you that the experience isn't real—or worse, tries to get you to stop the behavior that helps you cope with it—it only precipitates a further distortion of your experience of self. You end up negotiating with this place inside that feels so intensely strong that it can sometimes feel like a matter of life and death.

If an internal charge feels too strong, you'll do whatever it takes to dampen it, even if that means separating yourself from it or fragmenting your personality. In the moment, this strategy seems like a wise choice, and most likely it is. That highly charged experience that you disassociated and/or separated from, however, remains *within you,* isolated or compartmentalized. It's stuck in the past, by which I mean that *it cannot change its experience.* You can't integrate it, and when you feel its charge, it feels as if the exact same experience is happening all over again.

From that point on, until you're internally resourced enough to consciously engage and feel the experience within yourself from beginning to end, part of your *qi* or energetic flow will express itself this way. Disconnecting from the intensity dampens the charge, but you'll feel the consequences on all the other levels of your being. While part of you continues to move forward in time, the parts you've disconnected from remain in the same undeveloped, ongoing experience. As a result, the part of you that has moved forward can feel triggered by a charge from the undeveloped part and vice versa. This is usually an unconscious relationship, which is the reason true healing isn't always swift and easy, especially if you've functioned this way for many years.

Human beings are ingenious; we've constructed this artful dance as a way to keep ourselves functioning, and it works . . . up to a point. The dance also keeps us from living our full potential; the dance, after all, is a very limiting configuration. Fortunately, our desire to actualize and directly experience our full potential is one of our prime motivators. Our bodies often urge us toward integration through the pure physical exhaustion we experience from doing the same thing over and over. Eventually, we may become physically sick or suffer in other ways, which can precipitate further self-exploration in some of us. In other words, we eventually "get it" that we're stuck and spinning our wheels. Until we stop resisting—until we can own our current experience, exactly as it is—we can't create the conditions that could potentially allow us to perceive ourselves differently. Inner inquiry must always begin wherever we find ourselves, wherever we are at the moment. Ultimately, since it's our inherent birthright as humans, we long to be awake to and embody that which we are: divine.

We all function this way to varying degrees, and we'll continue to do so until we learn what we need to learn to consciously clear out the conflicts from our systems. As we gain momentum through this process, we integrate our experiences and open to the natural flow of life. This takes time. Each of us has a unique relationship to our beliefs, which directly impacts our healing process. Furthermore, some of us may need more time to integrate, depending on the degree of psychological fear or trauma we experienced in childhood, as well as the parameters of the belief we're functioning from.

A New Perspective on Addiction and Mental Illness

In general, I do not feel that labeling an individual an "addict" or "mentally ill" is helpful. When we use labels, we inflate and enliven the mental/emotional body by keeping energy caught in a highly charged mental construct. Because it's isolated from our physical awareness, it constantly regroups itself by providing stories in the form of thought patterns and associations that we react to, collapse into, and identify with. Our stories can go on endlessly as our physical charge builds and our mental/emotional discomfort increases. When we include our whole being in the inner exploration, our body wisdom summons our conscious awareness back to the precise place that our presence is needed by way of sensation.

Our awareness of sensate feeling is the bridge that connects our past history to the ever-present moment—this is where true and deep healing takes place.

Individuals are not addicts, nor are they defined by a label. By doing conscious and integrative work, you are waking up to identity in order to experience things as they actually are. *Your pathologies are entryways to the truth of your Being.* They are not issues to be fixed or changed; they are to be opened to and consciously and wisely experienced, so you may learn exactly what you need to learn. As soon as you take on an identity, you've opened one entryway and sealed the rest. You're working from an incomplete paradigm that interrupts the natural flow necessary for deep healing to take place.

Labels merely project a false sense of identity onto your delicate sense of self. As you reinforce the label over time, you instill a type of rigidity onto your physiology that keeps it all bound up. It's impossible to gain much momentum toward true healing when you limit your healing potential.

Who and what you are is beyond a label or a thought or a feeling. You don't have to awaken to it or become it. You are it. Healing is the process of making that distinction for yourself.

As I said earlier, there is wisdom in how you function, regardless of the obvious consequences. *You have addictive behaviors because the alternative is too intense.* It's imperative to really understand this. If you were to try to feel your internal experiences before you were ready—before your physiology was sufficiently integrated; before a skilled facilitator gave you the proper psychological, spiritual, and physical support; and before you had a safe enough physical environment to relax inward—you wouldn't be able to remain engaged with those internal experiences long enough to learn anything about your relationship to them. You'd also have a rough experience: caught in a loop of reactivity with very little awareness that it was even happening within you. Instead, you'd likely re-identify with it. Then you'd have to find a way to unconsciously diminish the intensity again, probably by returning to your addictive behavior or even creating a new one.

True healing is unfathomable. It's impossible to understand every inner dynamic that may present itself within your internal terrain. At times, you may come to a greater understanding that can widen your current perspective, but at other times, you may find value in not needing to understand your experience at all. There is an innate wisdom in letting something be as it is. The more comfortable you are with surrendering to the natural flow of life, the less you'll suffer and the more your inner distortions will heal.

When you peel back the layers of the onion in the healing process, it can feel intense and disorienting. However, if you're competently supported by someone who knows that "you" are not your story or your behavior, you'll feel respect, compassion, and validation for your current experience on *all levels of your being* without judgment or pressure to be someplace before you are authentically there. That's when deep healing and integration can naturally take place. You can then learn how to diffuse your physical inner charge a little at a time, so you can consciously be engaged with your full experience in order to move into and through it. This act can potentially clear the limiting experience from your system, which will allow you to authentically move with the natural flow of life and live within its rhythms.

When you're in an unconscious relationship with yourself, you cannot truly experience your inner landscape, which forces you to disengage from what you feel emotionally and physically. You become lost to your reactions, and your charge begins to build, which leaves you in an unconscious, reactive state in which the only thing you can do is unconsciously discharge that intensity. You must be engaged with the inner mechanics of your reactions in order to move from an unconscious pattern toward a direct and conscious connection with all the levels of your being. As you explore your relationship to your inner terrain—your beliefs, conditionings, reactions, physical sensations, blocks, and holdings—you'll feel a momentum that organically leads you deeper and deeper inside yourself. That's the result of being sincere and completely honest with yourself. That's the path of deep, authentic healing.

In order to be truly empowered, you need to move into your own awareness. The teachings in this book will mean very little unless you experience this for yourself. Even then, your experience will always be unique to you, not a set path outlined in any book.

Healing and Awakening without Using Labels

Healing and awakening always happen at their own pace—degrees, phases, and stages at a time, in a non-linear fashion. Every person is unique. Different people behave differently at different points in their development. To truly heal your distortion, you must look at the inner dynamics creating the behavior, not just at the behavior itself. Any addictive behavior is an adaptation; therefore, you must recognize the *validity* of that adaption. Inner exploration can provide an understanding of what benefits the behavior provides. It's important to not judge your behavior as right or wrong or healthy or unhealthy. That's just another story. Since the behaviors are helping you cope, it's important to resource yourself differently relative to your current experience of yourself. In essence, you need to validate for yourself that you are having the experience you're having and feel what it's doing for you, as opposed to telling yourself that your experiences are wrong.

It's very popular in the current treatment of addiction for therapists to work with clients to "break their denial." However, if you conform to *any* model of psychological health without understanding and feeling what the behavior is doing for you, then healing from the inside will not take place. *You must be able to directly experience your relationship to the inner mechanics as it relates to your behavior in the moment.* This experience internally resources you very differently. Without it, you'll have to unconsciously discharge your ever-increasing inner charge. Resourcing yourself differently awakens you to the cycle.

To accomplish true healing, we need a paradigm shift in the way that we as a society view addiction and mental/emotional imbalances. It doesn't help to look at ourselves as having a disease or disorder; we need to understand that we function a certain way to survive and endure internal experiences that are too intense to feel completely, openly, and honestly from beginning to end. Applying labels is much too superficial to bring about any real alignment with our true nature, which is the true source of all healing. *The truth of our essential nature is that we are not the label or the behavior.* The difference is subtle, yet very powerful.

In contrast, using labels can have value for some of us at certain points of our development, as long as we use them wisely. If we don't think of them as an all-or-nothing paradigm, we can use labels as a tool for inner exploration. For example, if we educate ourselves on the behaviors of addiction without reinforcing the identification with a label, we could possibly open ourselves to a better understanding of how we function. However, it's occasionally necessary to abstain from certain behaviors to keep ourselves or others safe. In this case, working with an outside-in perspective could be useful as a stepping-stone toward a more complete approach toward healing.

As a therapist, I recognize that modern psychotherapy only includes the mental/emotional levels of our being in its exploratory process, which limits its success rate for helping individuals genuinely heal their inner distortions from the inside. To encourage true healing to take place, psychotherapists have to include all the levels of our being: mental, emotional, physical, and spiritual. They're completely interconnected. Additionally, therapists interested in helping clients move inward on a deep level need adequate experience moving into and through their own unedited experiences. They must directly experience what the process feels like, or they'll be too intimidated to safely guide another inside to feel and engage their own conditioned expressions. It's a prerequisite for being able to competently guide another person. It's imperative, therefore, that our inner explorations include the physical body if we want deep healing and integration to take place.

Since many addictive behaviors are rooted in incomplete stages of early childhood development, it's essential that psychotherapists be able to properly support others as they move into and through the delicate emotional states that have mapped onto the entire physiology. How therapists approach and perform the exploration is of the utmost importance.

Working with the Physical/Energetic Component of Being

A healthy organism effortlessly flows with the movement of life, like a leaf floating downstream. It doesn't struggle with what is. Since nature is inherent in everything, you have to interact with it. How you do this is based on your relationship with it.

When you lose touch with the moment-to-moment direct experience of your true nature, your system gets blocked and your energetic flow becomes distorted. Consequently, your corresponding thoughts and behaviors become distorted. You lose touch with your natural rhythms. You enter a divided state in which you experience yourself as separate from the unified field of pure consciousness. Once this happens, you might grasp onto people, places, modalities, labels, behaviors, or activities as a way to lessen your discomfort. You might tighten or block your energetic flow.

Whatever you do (and everyone does something), you stop *feeling* as a way to accommodate those overwhelming inner charges. And once you stop feeling, you stop living in your body consciously. You may, for example, retreat into your head to function as a chronic intellectualizer. This of course creates a deep disconnection within the bodymind. Consequently, you lose touch with your physical experience, which causes you to feel even more ungrounded.

You also lose one of your most powerful tools for

self-healing and integration: a healthy flow between thinking and feeling. Once you override what you feel, you lose
the clarity to be able to validate for yourself what you're
feeling—you only know what you *think* you feel, which is
hardly the same thing. So you have to find someone to reduce
the inner charge, since most of your discomfort starts there.
You have to look outside yourself for clarity and validation
of your experiences.

Since you're unclear about what you're feeling, you fall
into an unconscious cycle: an inner charge continually builds
up until it eventually has to discharge itself. Then the cycle
keeps repeating. You remain unconscious not only of the discharge, but of the whole cycle.

The build-up and discharge are energetic. Energy doesn't
just evaporate; it has to go somewhere within your system.
A discharge often emerges as a repetitive thought pattern, a
physical behavior, or an emotional state or reaction that you
collapse into. Addictive behaviors are an expression of this
cycle. This is why you must work with the physical and energetic levels of your being when consciously engaging an inner
charge. This way, you can purposefully discharge the built-up
energy so you don't precipitate an unconscious result—like
falling back into the addictive behavior or becoming lost to
the experience.

To do this, to remain consciously engaged with your inner
charge, you use physical touch, breath and a body-felt sense
of awareness to take off the charge. This *begins* to re-establish a healthy energetic flow. Consequently, you're also able
to feel your experience within the physical body as it is. *Integration happens as you become conscious of that which you
were unconscious of before.*

I know many individuals who genuinely want to move into a more conscious experience of what is, but their internal charge is simply too great. I've found that when I work with them in a less direct manner to diminish their charge, they can be with their current experience more comfortably. This way of working gives them the ability to feel what before felt intolerable.

Emotions and Trauma Expressed within the Physical Body

Repressed emotions such as anger—as well as incomplete experiences such as trauma—get stored within your physical body. These repressed emotions and experiences can actually cause physical illness in addition to distortions on the other levels of your being. Trauma is essentially expressed as bound stress held within the physiology. A healthy system accommodates the genuine flow of emotion through physical sensation, so emotions aren't repressed, denied, or not consciously felt as physical sensation.

For example, if you feel anger, there might be a corresponding clenching in your chest or a tightness in your throat. When we consciously feel the sensations, the anger comes and goes without our needing to resist our experience. When we resist the full expression, the anger becomes a mental story, as opposed to a physical feeling. This is another reason why you must include the physical body in your inner exploration.

You cannot skip steps in the healing process to release stored trauma. It just doesn't work that way. For example, some psychotherapists do "anger release" work to force stuck energy to move out of the body. In these exercises, you yell at a chair or beat the floor with a pillow, screaming at every perceived perpetrator you can recall. The experience might feel silly, intimidating, or momentarily empowering. These artificial exercises are designed to conjure up the emotion stuck within you so it can be released from your system.

Compare this with the cut that heals itself: we set up the right conditions for healing to take place by cleaning and bandaging it. Nature knows how to do the rest, just as it knows how to heal a mental, emotional, or physical distortion. We only need to set up the proper conditions. By contrast, the anger release approach does nothing to allow the physiology to organically rewire itself so that you may come back into alignment with your natural rhythms, moment-to-moment. It's a trick, just another out-in approach. It's not true healing. You can't *force* healing to happen. True healing takes place organically from within you.

Those anger release exercises are supposed to help you look and feel healthier, having "rid yourself" of the offending or stuck emotion. The therapist assumes it's your repressed anger that's keeping you sick or unbalanced. While there is some truth to this assumption, the *process* of engaging and releasing the emotion is equally important. The natural path to true healing involves a seamless integration, so the process must facilitate integrating the new pattern of energetic flow back into the whole of your physiology. This recalibration takes time and can come with its own challenges.

You can't skip any steps. When the time is right for the next organic step in your personal and developmental process, it comes naturally. Until you have enough integration to challenge your personal beliefs about the suppressed anger—*and* until your physical body (and especially your nervous system) is able to handle the sensations of the charged energy flowing through blocks, your anger will continue to build up within you. You need to feel steady enough to consciously experience, engage, and support with compassion any undeveloped or disempowered aspects held within the personality. It takes a conscious, careful approach for true integration to occur, and it happens from the inside out.

As I stated earlier, healing happens within a certain window. You have to be able to remain engaged with your internal experience, moment-to-moment, without forcing a change or shift. This happens by degrees, so while working to integrate yourself, you have to respect that you've repressed a particular feeling for a valid reason. When releasing that emotion feels like the next organic step, you won't be able to hold it back. It becomes the next emerging layer of the onion. You'll naturally confront yourself and the inner experience. You won't need to be prodded. Until then, any forced experience just ends up being a discharge, not a true self-correction.

A Healthy Exploration with Your Inner Terrain

An undeveloped personality has much more power over you than you give it credit for. The human condition can be intense. It's so easy to identify with your beliefs, thought patterns, reactions, and associations—not to mention the intense waves of sensation you may have experienced at an early age. Most people have been conditioned to believe they know what a truly healthy individual looks like. This conditioning may have originally been taught or modeled to them by a parent or therapist, or it may have been instilled in them by our cultural norms. The point is that how you feel about yourself, to some degree, comes from some external source that aligns with your core beliefs about who and what you think you are.

Depending on your life experiences and individual personality, therefore, you're most likely adhering to some preconceived notion of *who or what* you should look like when you're healthy. The process of going deep within yourself to discover and engage what beliefs and conditionings you function from is vital if you want to live an authentic life.

Cultivating a healthy relationship with your inner terrain—and with all of life and existence—means not blindly following any one philosophy, theory, or model. There isn't a single modality or path that's the "right one." You may need many different models to help you explore, heal, and integrate your physiology, so one or even several, will be a more appropriate fit at specific times in your development. What is important, however, is how you use each modality in your integrative process. *If it becomes another model or label that you adhere to or identify with, then you are not using it wisely.* If you use it as a way to explore your inner dynamic, to learn how you function from that perspective, then you've developed a wise relationship that creates the potential for self-awareness and ultimately, deep healing and integration.

For example, if you use Jungian therapy as a tool to learn about your inner dynamic, but you can still explore it from another perspective—such as family systems theory—and find its value without grasping onto one or the other and identifying with it, then you're using that modality wisely. In the end, *you'll learn the story of how you've come to function the way you currently do.* This story can help you see, for the first time, the myriad ways in which you've become identified with your particular story and your inner reactions to it. The process isn't meant for you to identify with; it's meant to give you valuable information.

If you are attuned on a feeling level, you'll be able to feel within yourself when you're beginning to grasp onto something, be it a model or a label. As your flow begins to become blocked, you'll feel a constriction somewhere in your body. This is an example of why a healthy integration between thinking and feeling is so important.

Again, you might cultivate true health by using different models at different times in your process. The models may even contradict each other, yet still be very valid for you in that moment. You must discern for yourself what can potentially help you to consciously wake up to how you function.

There is an art to feeling and tracking your inner dynamic. Since you've most likely been functioning the same way for a very long time, you're unconsciously lost to that inner dynamic. While it takes time and practice to witness and feel the patterns within you, this process builds on itself, so you eventually gain the momentum you need to help you naturally evolve.

It's a rare person who can remain conscious on all levels of being. It's an ongoing process that takes tremendous sincerity, humility, discernment, contemplation, and truthfulness about your inner experiences and deeper motivations. Yet on this naturally evolving path, you can't help but gradually wake up and embody divinity. Remember: you are a spiritual being having a human experience, not the other way around.

In the next chapter, I'll examine how the physical body—like your conditioning—is simply an expression of your core beliefs.

CHAPTER 6

The Physical Expression
of Your Beliefs

As I said before, your beliefs create the way you perceive the world, so what you *experience* comes directly from what you *believe*. Your beliefs—along with the thoughts, emotions, associations, ideas, and reactions you identify with—become the blueprint for who and what you think you are. Therefore, you've been *conditioned* to think, feel, and behave as you do.

When you go unconscious, you're no longer moving with what is. This leaves you feeling divided. Your natural flow becomes distorted, which creates the blocks, holdings, and absences within the energetic system of your body. This in turn distorts your experience. Ultimately, you lose touch with your true nature *as it really is*. Worse, you're unaware of the distortions you've created. Yet your *relationship* with your thoughts, behaviors, emotions, and reactions is an expression of this dilemma.

The way you're configured internally—all the blocks and holdings, as well as the clear pathways—is a mapping of your beliefs. Once you understand how this works, it becomes easier to see that your physical body is really just an expression of your beliefs as well. Working organically with your energetic flow gives you the potential to help your bodymind naturally self-correct its distortions. Because everything is interconnected, *the very act of conscious exploration affects all levels of your being.*

Including the Body in Your Self-Exploration

To integrate your whole being, you *must* learn how to include the physical body in your inner exploration. It isn't enough to explore your experience only through the mental/emotional realm, as is done in modern psychotherapy. You must feel the physical sensations that correspond to the thoughts, emotions, and reactions you're experiencing in the moment, however subtle, exactly as they are. You have to track not only what you feel, but also when and how you go unconscious. This is actually one of the most commonly skipped steps in an individual's personal process, in part because it takes tremendous self-awareness.

It's easy to go unconscious (that is, editing your thoughts and reactions) when something feels uncomfortable or unacceptable, especially if you're caught in the surge of too much rising energy in the moment. When you resist your experience, it's common to change your thoughts or get caught up in analyzing or indulging them. When you notice that you're resisting what you feel, simply allow yourself to be with the resistance. Feel the corresponding sensation in your body. Don't force anything, just let it be what it is, while noticing your relationship to your thought patterns and reactions—in essence, *how you feel about what you think.* Observe your thoughts moving through and notice if you grasp onto them. Simultaneously, remain conscious of what sensations, holdings and absences you physically feel. Through this exploration, you'll discover whether you truly believe your thoughts.

Being vs. Doing

In the early days of my integrative work, I was waking up to how I had wired myself. I analyzed everything. I kept looking for a way out of what I was experiencing. The question I asked my teacher was always the same: "What should I do?" His reply was always the same: "Deborah, being is the doing." I couldn't get it! He watched me struggle while I tried to figure out what I should do, until I finally exhausted myself. Then I tried to emulate what I thought "being" looked like. Since I still resisted my experience as it was, I kept tying my internalized knot tighter and tighter.

One day, in response to a personal issue, I told my teacher that I felt I was being too passive in my approach and needed an action to take. His response to me was that *feeling is an action*. I sat there stunned! Suddenly, all those years of trying to mentally figure out everything I experienced felt like a waste of time. I realized in that moment that my life wasn't full of issues; it was full of experiences. It was impossible to figure everything out—and trying to was just the strategy or adaptation I used to keep myself from feeling experiences that felt unacceptable and intolerable. This was a huge revelation for me.

I come from the "self-help generation." We believe that if we don't like something about ourselves, we can change it. Just change our beliefs—or our behaviors—and we can experience ourselves in a whole new way. In the long run, we discovered, it didn't work. So there I was, exactly as I was before. I walked around for days, consciously watching my internal wiring (my conditioned responses), but this time I wasn't grasping onto it in the same way. My relationship to myself was evolving. I began to be still, breathe, feel, observe and listen. I didn't move away from what I didn't want to feel. I just let myself be. I'm not implying that I had come back into full harmony, but I was now able, thanks to my previous integrative work, to stay with an uncomfortable experience, exactly as it was. I could now consciously engage the stories being expressed within my bodymind.

I realized I had to consciously feel what I was experiencing, moment-to-moment, in order to reconnect with a fuller expression of myself. This brought me back in touch with my natural flow again. I was on a journey to become grounded in my being. I had forgotten what that experience felt like. It took me some time to re-establish the connection with my natural rhythms, but I could eventually feel the subtleties inside myself—so much so that I lost the desire to figure things out. I experienced a deep sense of reality as I began feeling what is and naturally moving with the flow of life. It became effortless to the point that I felt carried. I wasn't trying to control life any longer. I was simply being and living from that place of authenticity. I fell in love with what is.

Consciously Tracking Your Experience

We often don't recognize the spell we've fallen under. The strong charge that's locked within the system can feel intense and disorienting. If our experience is more than we can be with, we'll react and go unconscious. This leaves us caught in a loop created by our reaction to the thought patterns we've identified with—an experience we created, one that aligns with our beliefs. This internalized mode of function is how we believe our thoughts so fervently.

To observe and feel your experience, you must have the capacity to remain conscious (to be with what is). Fortunately, you have an ally: your body. You can learn how to use your physical body as a resource to diminish the charge you feel. Working consciously with your energy flow engages you with the direct physical expression of your beliefs, thoughts, and emotions. The work is powerful, so you must practice it responsibly. Once you put something into motion, you want to be able to accommodate it. Remember, your energy flow has been blocked for a very good reason, so you must be respectful of the blocks you encounter and the part they play in keeping you from feeling overwhelmed.

Start slowly when moving inward; learn to track and feel your inner flow. As your inner experience of yourself evolves, you'll be able to accommodate more. Over time, as you continue to work consciously, you'll learn more about how you function day-to-day. You'll learn to physically feel your experience, moment-to-moment, while observing what within you reacts and resists what is. As you move deeper still, you'll gradually awaken to how you identify with your beliefs, thoughts, emotions, associations, ideas ... essentially, your story. As you wisely open to your experience, you'll become both teacher and student as you learn about your relationship to yourself on every level of your being.

It takes commitment and focus to work this directly with

your energy system. Learning how to work directly with your body's flow patterns is a whole practice in and of itself. It's an intricate process that builds on itself, layers at a time, helping you reconnect the bodymind.

This process involves tracking and feeling the sensations of your unique energetic configuration—using your breath and physical touch. You can also use organic body movement, while making sounds that organically flow out of you, to encourage blocks and holdings to relax and the nervous system to recalibrate itself. This is an important stage in the integration of the bodymind; yet before you can do that work, you need to understand the dynamics.

This book isn't meant to provide all the tools you need to move through the stages and phases of deep awakening and healing, conscious embodiment, and whole being integration. The tools I do provide, if used appropriately, begin to resource you differently, which allows you to organically move inward into your next stage of psychological, physiological, emotional, and spiritual development.

This book gives you the foundation you need to begin moving deep inside yourself. Without this foundation, you won't be successful when you move into the beginning layers of this work. As you evolve, the foundation you create now will carry you forward. When you're ready to move inward and engage your terrain by working with your patterns of energy flow, you may need the support and guidance of a qualified facilitator or teacher. See Chapter 10 for more information about finding such a facilitator or teacher.

Each person moves inward at a unique pace. There are stages to this work, and while I have more tools for you as you move deeper inside yourself, it isn't appropriate for me to share them with you at this beginning stage. In this next section, however, I'll share with you some of the common stages that most individuals encounter along the way. Feel within yourself to discern whether or not each applies to you.

The Stages of Conscious Being, Integration, and Embodiment

To diminish your inner charge, you must learn to track how a charge builds up and then how to discharge it consciously. By *tracking*, I don't mean *analyzing* your body-felt sensations; I'm talking about really *feeling* them.

You first need to learn how to slow yourself down so you can consciously experience your internal reactions and sensations, along with your external behaviors. Slowing down creates the potential for you to learn about your relationship to your inner dynamic. As you observe and feel your experience, notice if you're analyzing or grasping onto it. *By consciously feeling what is, without grasping onto or pushing away, you experience where the infinite becomes manifest.*

This process brings your awareness to the places where you're energetically clenching or looping within your thought patterns and reactions. Being conscious creates the potential for your disowned energies to wake up and come back into the natural flow. Through this process, you experience evolving degrees of clarity. This becomes especially relevant if you're dealing with early infant trauma: which is essentially overstimulation or hyper-stimulation. (See Chapter 7 for more information about working with childhood trauma.)

Consciously feeling and exploring your physical blocks and holdings gives you a precise entry into your inner landscape. It's similar to the way a practitioner of Chinese medicine uses tongue and pulse diagnosis to see and feel the disharmony within you in order to prescribe the most effective treatment to bring you back into balance. The difference is, with this work, *you're* working directly with your inner dynamic.

Your consciousness evolves as you develop self-awareness and remain conscious of your experience, exactly as it is. Your bodymind releases old traumas and stresses that may show up as specific or non-specific fears, stagnations, binds, and holdings. With this newly developed awareness, you can consciously open to and feel your experience from beginning to end without the same overwhelming charge. This is only possible when you aren't completely lost to the experience, feeling distorted, compartmentalized, or overstimulated inside.

This work naturally grounds you, so you can remain conscious and increase your self-awareness. Remember this is an inwardly interactive process—don't expect it to feel linear.

Expressions of "Darkness" in the Unconscious

Some individuals believe that if they consciously explore a dark or shadow experience within themselves, they'll enliven or indulge it and get caught there. This fear can cause them to try to continuously create specific states of being, such as joy or ecstasy. In actuality, this hinders their spiritual development. As people spiritually evolve and mature, they expect to see the light *and* the dark. They want to understand their relationship to *both*.

When you open to pure consciousness, you can experience peace, love, expansion, joy, and beauty, but you can also experience the darker side of the unconscious, such as repressed emotions and associated images. When you're in an open state, everything seeks the light of consciousness. The goal of this work isn't to resist the fear or to indulge in it. It's a fine line, a razor's edge. You will, however, want to acknowledge what you are experiencing within yourself, while waking up to where you are grasping at feelings that you deem enjoyable or resisting experiences that feel uncomfortable. It's *here*, that you will notice how you are re-enlivening and re-identifying with your thought patterns. The goal is to become aware of *anything* that is stuck or in confusion of who or what it genuinely is, while compassionately validating, caring for, and supporting it's unique expression, so it may organically transform in the way that is right for it.

If you experience something so terrifying that you can't remain conscious of it, that experience of that fear gets imprinted in a nanosecond somewhere within your system. You may then form a number of conclusions and associations about the experience. Let's say hypothetically that you form a belief that the world is crude; therefore, it's not safe to be here. Yet it's a fact that you're here now. So now you have to create a series of adaptations to repress the awareness that you are alive and here, while finding ways to defend against your experience of the world as crude and unsafe. Since this belief maps onto the other levels of being, your energetic flow gets distorted as well. This directly affects your physical body. After some time passes—and momentum builds—you become accustomed to experiencing yourself in this limited way. This inner dynamic becomes your status quo. Yet it carries a monumental charge that was absorbed by your system much earlier and must now be managed—hence states of panic, hyper-stimulation, disassociation, addiction, fear, etc.

This can happen to anyone. This distortion remains stuck in the system, and we compound the problem because we come to believe that we *are* the experience (in the example above, an innocent victim in a crude world). We become identified with that story and its intense reactions. These conditioned reactions, the ones we've identified with, are what I refer to as "darkness."

I hope this example demonstrates how easy it is to go unconscious and experience a distortion with such intensity that you lose your connection to your true being. Healing and reawakening, therefore, is not as simple as releasing blocked energy or changing your thoughts. You really need to understand the broader picture to effectively heal and integrate.

The other thing to note about this process is that you don't have to try to bring up these dark experiences artificially. They organically present themselves when you're ready for the next phase or stage of your evolution.

Not All Fear Is the Same

As you move inward, you'll almost certainly encounter some fear. Most of us do. When it comes to fear, however, not all fear is the same. Over the years I've devoted to my process, I discovered two distinct types: psychological-based fear and spiritual- or existential-based fear. While they can appear the same at first blush, you must learn to differentiate between them so you know how to approach them. Because sometimes they come hand-in-hand, however, do your best to responsibly be with both simultaneously.

Moving fully into the spiritual or existential fear of *no-self* won't re-traumatize you, but moving completely into some psychological fear can. This process can be very dangerous and can set you back in your quest for true health. Do not underestimate the intensity of certain psychological fears! If you force your way in before you're resourced enough to accommodate the experience, you most likely will re-traumatize yourself, possibly to an even greater extent. The more intense the charge, the longer the process can take, so move inward a little bit at a time. Less is more, remember.

For some individuals, the process can get very intense when they come up against the fragmentations and splits within their bodymind. Again, the pace of this work depends entirely on you. Pay attention to what's in front of you and respect the cues you receive from your intuition. Do not force your pace and do not force yourself to open to experiences that are so intense that you will enliven them and get caught in them. Sometimes keeping a safe distance is what's needed. *Moving deeply inward before you can accommodate what you experience is counterproductive.*

There was a time in my evolution when I tried many different modalities and studied with many different teachers. On more than one occasion, I found myself at a workshop or spiritual retreat moving into experiences before I could accommodate them. The outcome wasn't pretty. I learned the hard way to trust my own experience and respect when it felt like it was too much to handle. I learned to keep myself safe from opening too much at any given time. I moved inward a little at a time, while validating and feeling all my experiences and discovering the boundaries where I could effectively remain engaged. This way, I never had more charge moving through my system than I could accommodate, so I wasn't enduring the fear of my experience.

That's not to say that it didn't feel intense. It did. But I was able to remain conscious of what I felt, degrees at a time, allowing the charge to trickle out. I found out for myself that many psychotherapists and spiritual teachers, though well intentioned, do not know how to work safely with hyper-stimulation and psychological trauma. I needlessly and repeatedly put myself in harm's way because I didn't know any better. Do your best to respect your unique experience and discern for yourself if your fear is spiritual-based or psychological-based.

Taking Complete Responsibility for Your Experience

As you do your inner exploration, ask yourself what's the deepest impetus behind all your actions. It's imperative that you be fully honest, so don't stop at your first answer. Continue to explore, feeling for the subtleties. You may not notice the deepest truth at first. Keep feeling deeper.

For example, if you lied to someone, dig to find the true reason for telling the lie. It's very easy to project what we unconsciously feel onto others without knowing it. Stay conscious and feel all the reactivity you experience as you do the exploration. Notice when you begin to feel agitated, annoyed, frightened, or bored. Then go back to the physical body and notice where you feel that charge. Begin to diminish the intensity by using physical touch, slow breathing and/ or movement. Don't get caught up in analyzing the situation or blaming anyone (including yourself). Remember that *you're just gathering information.*

This exploration leads to a better understanding of your relationship with yourself. As you experience more clarity, you may discover that the thread runs all the way back to your early childhood conditioning, or you may discover how your deepest impetus relates to your beliefs. With practice and the proper support, you can connect the dots to learn how this new information relates to all your current relationships. You'll develop clarity about how you project your unconscious beliefs and associations onto other people, as well as onto the world at large. You'll gain more insight into what life consistently reflects back to you. That's what it means to be a co-creator of your life experiences. *Eventually, you awaken to the direct experience that ultimately every experience is self-created.*

Undertake this work with compassion for yourself. Accepting complete responsibility for your inner experience cannot happen if your motivation is to shame or punish yourself. Complete responsibility, first and foremost, comes from genuinely understanding the honest reasons behind your actions. Only then can you understand your relationship to the beliefs and conditionings that led to those actions. As you work through the layers of the onion—learning more about how you function; feeling into the blocks, holdings, and absences within your body; validating for yourself that your experience is happening within you as it is; and reducing the charge by using touch, breath, and movement—you'll move naturally into the next stage of your inner development. This is how you care for yourself; this work resources you differently.

Waking Up within the Story

This work involves giving validity to everyone's story, and you'll likely find multiple stories going on within you simultaneously. After all, life is a paradox. Try not to get too invested in any one story. Remain compassionate, curious and interested; yet understand that each one is only a story, even while it feels very real for you. Also, realize that *you are not the story*. In other words, the story does not define who and what you are. Notice the subtleties as you move inwardly on deeper levels. Allow the story to organically open you to fuller expressions of being. Observe where you've identified with a story as well as where you've been defined by your history—for example: my parents didn't want me, so I must inherently be a bad person.

We all have a very concise story that we brought with us into this life, based on who and what we believe we are. Our life experiences are the expressions of a story that we've become caught up in and lost to. Most of us experience this inner dynamic unconsciously. It's the filter through which we perceive everything. When we identify with our reactions and associations, it reinforces our story again and again.

We're caught in a closed loop. It's like being inside a particle accelerator: we develop tunnel vision. Inside the accelerator, our belief and its associations—like particles in an accelerator—gain momentum as they go around and around. As a result, we forget who and what we are outside the narrow perspective of the tunnel. It all feels very real, and in a way, it *is* real.

Here's another example. Let's say you've worn eyeglasses with yellow lenses your whole life. Everything you see has a yellow tint to it, but you never realize that it's the lenses that are yellow-tinted, not the objects of your perception. You've become accustomed to experiencing yourself and the world in this limited way. Others see that your lenses are yellow, but you can't imagine anything different since this is how you've come to know and experience yourself. It's all *you* know. This is how your instilled conditioning works.

Everybody on the planet does this—until they wake up to how they currently function and are no longer unconsciously lost to the identification with their belief systems and thought patterns. Even then, no one is immune to going unconscious again. This process isn't as simple as trading one belief for another. To meet your story at its deepest core, you work from where you are and allow nature to reveal it to you. You embody your experience of this truth, degrees at a time.

Each phase or level of consciousness has its own reality and must be respected. Each phase brings with it its own set of experiences, so be honest about where you are, right in this moment, no matter what level or phase you find yourself in. To do this, your deepest sincerity is required. You can control nothing. Learn to be still, listen, observe, feel, and consciously interact with what life shows you. It's as natural as breathing. Your relationship to the movement of life, like your breath, takes on a natural rhythm—or not, depending on the degree to which you can surrender.

As I've said throughout this book, if something feels like it's too much for you, then it is. Respect that. You can't rush this work. If you can't accommodate an experience, then you need to gain experience by doing more conscious inner exploration, exactly as you are. This can lead to fuller degrees of physical embodiment so you can experience yourself more fully and directly. Understanding your relationship to your story is an essential part of the healing and awakening process. Eventually, you discover that your experiences are direct expressions of your core belief or story.

Successfully Working with Your Story

Your thought patterns are circular, as in a closed loop. They go round and round, telling you many similar versions of the same story. It's very easy to lose yourself to this inner dynamic. Consciously tracking and working within the physical/energetic realm of existence can teach you how to *not* follow your story exclusively.

If, for example, you're used to having a backlog of energy held in your upper chest and head, you may often feel speedy or overstimulated to the point that you stop consciously feeling anything else because you're already maxed out. This becomes your norm, your adaptive mode of function. The constant chatter in your head—the cyclical thinking and overstimulation of your brain—keeps you from feeling your experience. It also blinds you to how you react to your inner and outer worlds, which as I've explained is just a function of your underlying beliefs and conditionings that create your core story.

By looking at how you function in the context of the whole, you may notice that all the stuck hyper-energy circulating in your head seems to give you the ability to function without having to feel the conscious distress of your inner beliefs. This adaptive mode of functioning is self-limiting, but it lets you keep going ... at least until it stops working. In other words, it comes at a price.

To move from an unconscious mode of functioning into a conscious mode of functioning, you need the proper support and tools to withstand the destabilization process that can occur while you do the work. In essence, you're deconstructing the structures of your personality and the various ways it interconnects within your physiology. It's not always comfortable to go through a self-correction. Because you always wake up within your current experience of yourself (your distress) instead of where you hope to wake up (beyond your distress), you may need a facilitator's support to effectively engage your distorted experience all the way to completion. Proper support allows you to consciously feel the experience without further re-enforcing the identification with your reactions.

As you shift from one experience into another, it might feel like the rug is being pulled out from under you. Your inner configurations were developed for survival—they were meant to protect you from an inner intensity that you just didn't have the capacity to accommodate. If you're unaware of what's going on inside you, you may think you're making progress with your personal development, only to get smacked in the face by another layer of your conditioning.

Life reflects the unconscious relationship you have with yourself right back at you again and again until you can remain consciously engaged enough to learn what you are meant to learn. So even when you *think* you're avoiding yourself, you really aren't, not in the context of the bigger picture. You might be avoiding one small thing in the current moment, but nature won't let it rest. Your unconscious beliefs will be reflected back to you through your life experiences. *You will have the experiences you're meant to have.* In the end, you have to deal with things as they present themselves in the only way you can. The saying, "no wine before its time," is very true in this regard.

As you integrate more and more, each layer you feel and engage becomes part of the conscious whole. Thus it supports you as you engage the next layer. On one hand, the process is effortless when you're connected to your natural inner rhythms and organically flowing with the movement of life. This is your natural state of being. Simultaneously, it takes some effort to establish momentum as you move into a healthier relationship with each layer of your conditioning. This is because you've become accustomed to living outside the natural flow of life. As you restore balance within yourself by normalizing your inner flow and tracking your current physical, mental, and emotional distortions, you effortlessly rest inward on deeper and deeper levels, awakening to the seamless integration of your whole being. As you eventually come to understand that the story is happening *within you* and that you aren't *defined by it*, you can take responsibility for your experiences. This in turn shifts your relationship with how you've unconsciously projected your disowned experiences onto others. As I said in the previous chapter, you'll eventually experience yourself as a conscious co-creator of life and existence, feeling the subtleties of your experience deep within yourself.

This work must be undertaken with the utmost sincerity. You can't fake your way through it. Your inner resonance will always be reflected back to you.

Freedom from Belief Systems

As you move inward through the layers of your experiences, peeling back the layers of the onion, those deeply entrenched distortions make their way to the surface. Once an experience is close enough to the surface, you can potentially *move into and through it,* while feeling it transform, without losing yourself to it and going unconscious again. Since the charge around it has greatly diminished, you now potentially have more clarity with which to experience not only the expression of the underlying belief, but also your relationship to it. You've replaced the charge with evolving degrees of self-awareness and integration throughout your physiology. You can accommodate more of your own natural flow too.

This might be the time to challenge your currently held belief in order to make sure no other aspects within you are also an expression of the belief. Move inward and feel any leftover reactivity within you. If you can stay present, for example, while making up mock scenarios that you'd have typically felt reactive about, then you can be certain that your relationship to that belief has shifted and it's been released from your system. If you discover that you're still reactive, then remain engaged with this place inside yourself, validating and feeling your experience along the way. Possibly, there are more layers for you to move through as you learn about your relationship to your reactivity.

When I engaged an inner reaction in my past, my teacher used to say that I needed to "stay present in order to feel the chameleon move on the quilt." When a chameleon sits on a busy quilt, it blends in and you can't see that it isn't part of the quilt. But if you remain present and open, feeling the subtleties of your experience, you'll see both the chameleon and the quilt. The same is true for dealing with your distortions.

To enable your integration (and your soul's development), you must be able to physically track and feel the myriad ways you've identified yourself as something other than divine. Including the physical body in your exploration gives you the capacity to challenge those old grooves of conditioning directly. *As you're able to feel the subtleties of your experiences in the physical body and track them, you establish new pathways.* It's literally like a snowplow clearing the roads that were buried beneath the snow. Yet when you're lost to your conditioned responses, you believe that roads covered in snow are how roads are *supposed* to be. The distortion or karmic impressions are that convincing.

Remember, the way to work with a belief isn't to try to change it, but to learn more about your relationship to it. It's your relationship with the belief that changes, not the belief itself. To learn about your current relationship to a belief, track your experience as it is, moment-to-moment, feeling the nuances that reverberate on all the levels of your being. This exploration has to be done gently and organically.

You can't engage a belief by imposing your will on it, by trying to change it, or by affirming a new belief. It doesn't work that way. If you try to force your will onto a belief and its conditioned responses, you'll remain in the clutches of your distortions. Instead, you have to allow the wisdom of the bodymind to align in a harmonious way. This process is vital.

In Western culture, we've been conditioned to believe that we have free will over our inner and outer experiences—that if we don't like what we see around us, we can actively seek to change it. Exercising our free will without learning how to physically feel and remain conscious of how we function moment-to-moment merely continues our inner disconnect.

Without a conscious relationship to our inner world, we've skipped a step. We may believe we can manipulate nature by having power over it, but in the end, we just tie ourselves up in bigger knots, losing touch with the only true mechanism for healing: nature and our healthy relationship with it. It's important to understand how to exercise our free will, without going unconscious to our current experience.

Recalibrating the Nervous System and Establishing New Wiring

Explore each physical or psychological block with the utmost care. It's easy to get stuck there, circling round and round in the experience, feeling as though it's happening again. Remember to keep yourself in the physical here-and-now, while remaining conscious of what you're experiencing internally. Over time, as the charge lessens and you culti-vate more clarity and integration, you'll gain the potential to organically move fully into and through your experience. As this happens, you'll move into *co-consciousness*—where you're able to witness both experiences (your experience of the distortion and your experience of the present) simulta-neously. Moving through the layers, you'll see and feel the *original experience*, but since you've cultivated a different relationship to your beliefs and conditionings, you won't be quite as identified with the original reactivity. It can feel as though you're *seeing it for the first time, with clear eyes*. Over time, you'll find it much easier to move into your experiences as your system discharges the backlog of rising energy and re-calibrates your nervous system, one layer at a time. That's when you'll know and feel the process is really working.

You eventually come to understand that your relationship toward yourself and others—as well as the issue you're exploring—has been a function of your self-limiting beliefs. This is why it's important to stay with an experience until completion, until you no longer feel reactive to it. This means it's released itself from your system. The inner transformation and transmutation that has taken place has allowed for a different perception of reality. How long this takes is different for everyone. If you're highly reactive, your process may take longer since your wiring has burned some deep grooves within your physiology. Essentially, you need time to repair those grooves and re-establish a fuller connection with yourself. When you feel more awakened within yourself, you'll see that your reaction never really identified who and what you truly are.

You might still bump up against some aspect of this same distortion at a later date. Ultimately, you never know. The stages of your development aren't completely linear; they can overlap. There aren't any concrete steps in this work because the human physiology is dynamic, not static. Movement is built into the structure of existence. Evolution takes place whether we resist the flow or not. As you're able to move into an experience physically, meaning you can really feel it in your body, you'll feel it begin to self-correct. It isn't something someone else can do to you; rather, it's something you have to experience for yourself. It happens within you through your conscious awareness and interaction.

As you observe, feel, compassionately validate, and engage your current configuration and its many expressions, an energetic current begins to move through areas of your system that had previously been blocked. This can take a little time for the nervous system to adjust to, physically and emotionally, since you aren't used to having such a full relationship with yourself. Sometimes it can take months or even years for the re-calibration to complete itself. As my teacher used to say, "The wiring is there, but you're not used to running current through it." Go slowly. This part of the integration process can feel very uncomfortable for some people. I've had many moments over the years when I felt like I was plugged into a light socket as more current moved through my system than I could comfortably tolerate. This physiological shift can create head pressure, sleepless nights, agitation, disorientation, shakiness, speediness, body aches, tremendous heat in the system, brain fog, and a general sense of feeling unwell.

When this happens to you, make organic sounds and use touch, breath, organic movement, and even stretching to allow your nervous system to accommodate the new "voltage." Keep the upper body and top of the head open so the rising energy won't become backlogged. Simultaneously, remain grounded by keeping your legs engaged. Some of the ways you can do this is by rubbing your head, face, eyes, neck, and chest to smooth out the energy flow so it doesn't feel as intense. Use long strokes on your arms and legs, while crisscrossing your hands over your chest and torso. You can also go for slow walks, roll on your spine, or gently go into a squatting position, moving up and down and then twisting your upper torso from side to side as you stand. Feel how *your* body wants to move. *Allow yourself to feel all the new experiences that emerge.* You may find that old experiences are brought to the surface so you can consciously experience them through to completion and move them out of your system. Remember not to analyze or grasp onto your experiences. As I said earlier, you always experience the opposite of where you are, so the more you're integrated, the more you're going to feel.

As you do this work, you'll feel your old blocks and stagnations release. A new experience of yourself—your natural expression of being—moves in and becomes embodied. It's always been there, but it was hidden in the same way that clouds hide the moon. When it reveals itself, you'll feel a different *quality* to your being.

As I said, it will likely take time to integrate this "new you" into your personality, nervous system, and the rest of your physiology, which is why the process is more like peeling the layers of an onion than racing to a destination. Remember that this journey looks different for everyone. How I look when I'm more integrated is going to look very different from how you'll look. That's the beauty of the human experience: each of us is as unique as a snowflake.

When you're met and supported where you are in the moment, it helps you, the adult—as well as the inner, undeveloped aspects within you—to feel validated, which in and of itself can discharge some of your built-up inner intensity. When you can consciously feel and explore, with compassion, all the inner aspects held within the charge, not only do you learn how to work within its inner mechanics, but you also recalibrate and experience yourself more comfortably and clearly.

Many of your inner blocks are isolated expressions that are unable to have a different experience. They can only do the same thing over and over. Hence, they color your experience of yourself—you identify yourself through them—although usually unconsciously.

Feeling vs. Talking

Sometimes, talking about your experience doesn't shift anything within your physiology, but after five minutes of feeling into the corresponding physical sensation (and being really honest about what you experience), your physiology can come back into balance in a way you won't be able to put into words. Often, words are just a superficial discharge, a way to discharge the intensity of an inner charge, until you're able to remain engaged with what you feel. Intellectual banter can merely be a way you keep yourself from genuinely feeling what's underneath. The most efficient way to become integrated is to learn to accommodate deep stillness and silence and observe what moves upward through your awareness. Consciously *feel* inside yourself, opening deeper into the subtleties, while allowing moments of conscious verbal expression.

As you slow down, you can connect the dots and learn how past experiences have conditioned you to accept your current experience of yourself. If you can do this, you'll have an opportunity to see how you currently function from a different perspective. As you become more conscious of your inner dynamic, you become more facile at *feeling* for the most optimal way to work with yourself. Then you'll sense which path best leads to a self-correction. The manner in which you do your inner exploration is the deciding factor in how successful you'll be in your integration.

Working with thoughts and emotions through the physical body can ground you in the present moment while diminishing your inner charge. The story your conditioned mind tells you may have nothing to do with what's happening in real time. You can follow your thoughts endlessly, especially when they're pregnant with emotion *and* when they feel so very real and familiar. While it's important to acknowledge all aspects of what is, you must develop an ability to verify whether the thoughts really are in line with the here-and-now.

For example, let's say you're feeling rejected by your partner. You follow your thought patterns, which get you all worked up because of the story they tell you. Then you notice the only thing that's real in the moment is that you're sitting on your bed in your room, alone. That's what's really happening. This reality can help keep your thoughts in perspective. That's not to say that the internal experience you're having isn't happening. It is! Both experiences are happening simultaneously. However valid the story might be to the undeveloped or incomplete aspects within you, it's still just a story. If you slow yourself down enough to remain conscious, you may realize that your reaction is a story too. Your experience, your thoughts about it, and the story they tell are all valid. And they all can provide valuable information about how you currently function—although they are in no way indicative of your essential Self.

Since your beliefs and conditionings are expressed in a multilayered fashion, the same issue or theme can continuously come up, as you explore layer by layer. This doesn't mean all your previous work was in vain. It means that you're exploring the issue at deeper and deeper levels. You can't explore it at a deep level unless and until you explore it at the more superficial levels. It's a process.

Stay with your experience as it is. Do your best to not skip steps. Work from the knowledge that at the depth of your being, all is well. You don't need to *change* anything about yourself. Doing your inner exploration and being with your full experience as it is will reveal your beliefs, reactions, and identifications. The places within you that are "caught in confusion about who and what they truly are" will awaken, and the trapped energy will be restored into the natural flow of consciousness. Best of all, through this process, you'll develop Self-awareness: an evolutionary step.

Along the way, however, you are likely to come up against many obstacles. In the next chapter, I discuss some of them.

CHAPTER 7

Deconstructing the Many Facets of Conditioning

As you do the work and move through the layers of your conditioning, you'll notice a theme or story that plays out in your experiences. Exploring your relationship to this theme can produce tremendous self-awareness, especially as you move deeper, bringing you up against the subtleties of your experience. Being able to look objectively at your outer story while moving inward to physically feel your current experience moment-to-moment brings clarity and integration as you connect the dots.

Observing when you go unconscious is an important part of cultivating self-awareness. To bring about the integration of your bodymind, you'll want to wake up, to become conscious, which eventually leads you to experience what you do when you go unconscious. To get to that point, ask yourself questions during your inner explorations. Ask where you feel reactive inside. What are the physical sensations in your body? What associations do the sensations evoke in you? What are the thought patterns that have caught you recycling the same things over and over again? What conclusions have you reached, based on your idea of who or what you think you are?

As you consciously feel your way through the layers of your experience, you'll wake up to how you're caught looping in an unconscious relationship with your mental and emotional patterns. It's that relationship that keeps you further identified with your story. It also keeps your physiology locked in the same habitual patterns, which express themselves as the blocks, holdings, and absences you experience within your bodymind. These patterns limit your perspective, as well as your ability to physically accommodate a fuller experience of yourself. To find relief, you create adaptations that allow you to exist more comfortably as you unconsciously discharge the stress you feel within. However, *relief is not the same thing as deep physiological healing. There is a difference between your being "well adjusted" versus "free and clear" of your distortion.* As the pattern self-corrects, you're less reactive to the same story; therefore, you're no longer looking for relief by discharging its energy.

You'll function this way to varying degrees as you cultivate a physiology that naturally allows you to fully surrender to the natural flow and movement of life. As I stated earlier, you function as you do because the alternative is too intense, even if the way you now function limits your true potential. Your inner distortions remain stuck until you're resourced enough to experience them consciously and re-integrate that energy back into your system. Only then will they release and find completion.

Your particular theme or story and its corresponding emotion will continue to keep you company as you move inward through the layers of conditioning and as you consciously experience your inner terrain—on *all* levels of your being. So *how* you move inward becomes vital. As you consciously feel your current experience, you slowly cultivate a physiology that allows you to seamlessly experience all levels of your being. In other words, as you directly "experience" your divine nature as "no-thing" and everything, you'll also experience your individual expression through your very human and very physical journey.

Working with the Physical Expression of Conditioning

When you include the body in your self-exploration you must feel for holdings, blocks, or absences on the physical level. By feeling and observing your energy flow, you may notice, for example, that certain areas in your body feel tight, numb, or absent altogether. As you bring your awareness to your body and are able to feel where you are tight, clenching, or flowing, you send a different signal to your body. This new signal lets the bodymind know that you are ready to receive flow through those previously blocked areas. Through this exploration of what you're feeling, your emotional as well as your physical experience of yourself can shift considerably. Without a direct connection to the physical, all an emotion can do when you unconsciously experience it is to continue discharging and regrouping itself internally. You leave it no choice; the energy has to go somewhere within the system.

For example, if you believe you aren't safe in the world, then you'll perceive life through this very specific lens. Simultaneously, this belief is expressed on the physical level. Your body may tighten up and block your energetic flow (your life force) so you won't have to fully experience yourself being in the world moment-by-moment. This clenching keeps your conscious reactivity to a minimum. So even though this block distorts your energetic flow and causes mental, emotional, and physical symptoms, it also does something for you: it helps you function in the world without directly experiencing constant fear.

The dynamic unfolds this way: when you minimize the energetic flow through your pelvis and lower abdomen, you feel less grounded. As a result, you may feel as if you are cut off from the earth's energy. Your lower body feels blocked and disconnected, which leaves your whole physical body weakened. This feeling reinforces your belief that it isn't safe for you to be here. It also keeps you from consciously feeling the intensity of your reactivity (in this case, fear) to your belief, which is not a small thing.

This example shows not only how your physical body expresses your inner beliefs, but also what your adaptations can do for you. As uncomfortable as a blocked pelvis can make you feel, you'll likely find it more tolerable than consciously feeling your ongoing reaction to your belief and constantly waking up within it. In other words, it's highly intolerable to consciously feel yourself physically incarnated when you believe it's unsafe.

This dynamic is not, however, a problem to be fixed; it's merely valuable information for you to become aware of. As I've said before, awareness of your inner landscape is the means by which you learn more about how you currently function. You still have to work with this internal configuration—but not to force it to change. While you might assume that a different experience would be easier to feel, if you can't be with *this* experience consciously moment-to-moment, you won't be able to be with an alternate experience either.

Because everything in nature is interconnected, the scenario described above affects your entire physical body as well. Now your whole physiology becomes distorted to some degree, and you lose your true connection with your natural rhythms. As one layer of your relationship to your core story self-corrects, the next layer of the distortion reveals itself. This in turn affects your psyche. *When a distortion self-corrects, it creates the potential for further self-correction on the other levels of your being.* However, you don't have to engage every little distortion on every single level to fully integrate an experience. That would make the process endless. Instead, it's like a cascade or avalanche: one small piece starts everything in motion. Eventually, you gain momentum.

Multiple Layers, Multiple Perspectives

When you work from a multilayered perspective, you learn to start exploring from what you're currently experiencing in the moment. One of my teachers used to say, *"In nature, there are equally valid, yet simultaneously contradictory realities. Wisdom is knowing which reality makes the most sense to align with in the moment."*

Working this way means not following a rigid set of rules or steps. Allow yourself to consider different perspectives, different realities. This can feel challenging, especially if you want to stay only with what feels comfortable. Be open and curious. Working from only one psychotherapeutic model or one healing paradigm keeps you in the clutches of your holdings since you consistently experience only one perspective. To naturally flow with the movement of life, you can't rule out *any* perspectives. While every perspective won't help your physiology self-correct, by following your natural rhythms, you'll eventually find the modality or perspective that opens your awareness in that moment.

When doing this exploration, keep in mind that every experience along the continuum is valid. One experience is not better than another. Even if one reality isn't the wisest to align with in that moment, that doesn't mean it isn't valid. Paradoxically, even though every reality or perspective is valid, that doesn't mean it's necessarily true or even right for you. Be aware that you have to make a distinction here and that you must awaken and perceive this seemingly paradoxical expression of existence through a felt direct experience because it's much too confusing for the intellect alone.

The focus of your exploration isn't to analyze anything or to make someone or something wrong. *Just notice everything as it is.* You must be completely honest with yourself. Don't hide any response, regardless how slight it may seem. Allow your inner wisdom to guide you. Notice if you find yourself looking for an end result. Observe how your inner defenses work, as well as when and how you become reactive to other perspectives. Take note if anything within the exploration makes you feel uncomfortable. If you feel particularly reactive or righteously indignant in response to any perspective or experience, notice how this reactivity feels in your body. How do you hold your body in this moment? Can you feel your charge? A charge can indicate a conflict within you.

Cultivate a physiology that can move naturally from one reality or perspective to the next in your inner exploration. Allow yourself to "change channels" with regard to what you're doing. For example, if you're reading a book, get up and move your body from time to time. Do something that uses another one of your senses, such as listening to music.

Encourage your various sensory channels to remain open. Remember, they are interconnected. Changing channels with awareness keeps you from stagnating. This mode of functioning aligns you with the natural flow of life. As a result, you'll experience yourself becoming more aware and more seamlessly integrated.

If done properly, this kind of exploration can give you the ability to become aware of when you blindly adhere to one perspective or reality. The process is delicate, so be mindful: it's easy to get caught in self-righteous attitudes. I'm merely skimming the surface regarding this type of exploration. It takes time, commitment, complete honesty, and sincerity to move deeply inward and re-establish a healthy relationship with your whole being.

Using Relationship Consciously to Engage Your Inner Dynamic

Another way to learn about yourself is to review your external relationships. If you pay attention, they can reveal how you function within yourself. Since other people have different perspectives on life, they can give you the opportunity to see where and when you rigidly function from your self-limiting beliefs. Again, this can feel challenging, so be easy with yourself.

For example, in a relationship with a significant other, we tend to go unconscious when our experience feels uncomfortable. However, before we even realize that *we* had an internal reaction, we typically focus outwardly on our partner's behavior and cast the blame there for why we feel uncomfortable. As a result, we may do one of two things: demand that our partner change, or we shut down and pull away, telling ourselves we deserve someone better. We can convince ourselves that our discomfort comes from outside ourselves. This can happen in every type of relationship, whether it's with a significant other, close friend, parent, sibling, or co-worker. When we feel reactive, our knee-jerk reaction is to project our disowned experience onto our perception of "other." The closer the relationship, the more challenging it is to clearly see our own projections. Therefore, we may sometimes avoid having a relationship with ourselves by avoiding deeper relationships with others.

If you want to be awake, you have to be willing to learn all about how you currently function: tracking how and when you go unconscious, as well as learning how going unconscious genuinely serves you. A good way to do this is to consciously use your relationships as a window through which you can see how you react with others, feel the emotions that get stirred up, and take responsibility for your own experience. Creating conscious relationships means that not only do you feel all of your experiences and take responsibility for them, but you also let others have their own experiences. If this idea makes you feel uncomfortable, then that gives you information about how you currently function.

Again, be easy on yourself. It can be challenging, for instance, to wake up from an identity of being the "nice person" you thought you were to one who's not always so nice. The more invested you are in remaining unconscious, the more challenging it will be to see your blind spot. Seek support from a qualified facilitator if you need it.

Here's another example. You may feel judgmental or sarcastic in response to how you feel about another's experience, but if you hide that reaction from yourself, that means you are going unconscious. You need to observe and consciously engage this inner dynamic so you can awaken the "formed energy" that's caught up in it. In other words, you may want to explore your inner landscape to look for your real motivations, the reasons why you react and go unconscious in this situation. Yet you wouldn't even have known to look if you hadn't consciously used your relationship as a learning tool about yourself.

Infant Dynamics and Early Childhood Trauma

Working with the bodymind is especially important when you're dealing with infant dynamics and early childhood trauma. The *reactive infant bodymind* is an imprint or inner dynamic that gets emotionally, psychologically, spiritually, and physically embedded in you as an infant during your early development, from the in-utero experience to the first four to five years of your life. Although trauma at older ages can have severe consequences as well, early childhood trauma occurs during the most developmentally important ages.

Here's what happens: when infants encounter stress, they experience that stress as an inner charge that feels all encompassing. It distorts their limited experience of themselves. Since infants can't reduce the stress on their own, they look externally, to their caregivers. If the caregivers don't diffuse the charge for the infants within a reasonable amount of time—by picking them up, speaking to them with a comforting tone, or making some kind of physical, emotional, and/or eye contact—the unresolved overstimulation creates a highly charged infant bodymind that's experienced as a life-

or-death situation. Consequently, the infant is thrown into a survival polarity. Infants can't deal with such a situation, so they have no alternative but to split off, fragment, or disassociate within themselves, which can cause the experience to become a type of frozen imprint on the emotional, psychological, spiritual, and even physical levels.

The quality of the caregiver-infant relationship sets the stage for what I've called the *reactive infant bodymind*. As the infant rapidly develops, the nervous system and cognitive abilities develop as well. Although the infant eventually develops chronologically, part of their energy remains stuck developmentally in a highly charged, distorted experience.

Because it's impossible to have a perfect childhood, this kind of thing happens in varying degrees to *everyone*. Have you ever suddenly felt an unconscious reaction to someone or something that seemed irrational or came out of nowhere? Have you felt stuck in a relationship dynamic that seems similar to your last one, but keeps hooking you in even as you observe yourself doing the same thing again and again, regardless how cleverly you've tried to change your thoughts and behaviors? If so, it's quite possible that the *imprinting* held within your reactive infant bodymind has become enlivened unconsciously. You can't understand it because you have no way to connect the dots back to your early childhood. You would need to be able to physically feel your emotional experiences in order to do that.

This reaction can feel very confusing. As an infant, you didn't have a vocabulary to express yourself. Your experiences were all encompassing. While the mirror in front of you reflects an adult, the strong inner reactions you feel come from a limited childhood development. Despite having a mature body, you've walled off part of your infant body-mind experience. As a result, you may *never* feel quite right within yourself. It's because part of your energy is frozen in a highly charged infantile experience. Consequently, you're never able to feel truly connected to your whole being. You can never fully rest into yourself. You feel divided.

This inner disconnect or split can precipitate an episode of panic. Typically, you intellectualize your reaction. If you've been a longtime seeker of self-improvement or spirituality, you might pull an adaptive tool out of your toolbox to try to make sense out of something that ultimately can only make intellectual sense, but not emotional and physical sense because it doesn't reach to your reactive infant bodymind, where the real convincing needs to happen. In essence, all you can do is endure and seek ways to overcome your intense charge. When this conditioning becomes enlivened, you have no way of comprehending that you're having this experience *within* yourself, so you can't give yourself what you need to feel calmer and more self-referred. To compensate, you look outside yourself for a signal that you're all right, just as you once did as a child with your caregiver. It's like having a secret life going on inside you, but you can't consciously connect to it.

Here's an example. I once had a client who came to my practice because she kept experiencing a fear of "forfeiting herself" in her intimate relationships. Her previous facilitators taught her to artificially create new behaviors in order to change the patterns of her mind—in essence, to cut new grooves into her brain. Her goal was to change the way she thought about herself when she was in an intimate relationship so she would stop focusing exclusively on taking care of the other person. Yet every time she related to someone in a deep way, she felt she lost sight of herself and her own needs.

A bright and determined woman, she enjoyed great success in her corporate career, which left part of her feeling very capable. She proved she could take care of herself financially, and she earned the admiration and approval of her peers. She'd hoped the recognition would prove she was a deserving, lovable, and capable adult—and not the needy, frightened, dependent child she sometimes experienced herself as.

Whenever she got involved in an intimate relationship, however, she unconsciously experienced the charge imprinted onto her nervous system from energy caught in an undeveloped infantile configuration. In other words, she felt tremendous distress and had no idea why or how to take the charge off. In fact, she felt blindsided. The energy was caught in an unconscious, reactive, internal loop, and she had no way to access it.

So while others saw her as a capable and even highly functioning woman, deep inside, she felt caught in an ongoing experience of great fear. She had tried to "appear healthy and functional," yet when she showed up in my office, she felt disconnected from herself. Worse, she was losing hope that she might ever feel whole. I explained to her that trying to emulate a healthy experience based on other people's out-in advice was keeping her disconnected from her authentic rhythms—in essence, her genuine experience.

As I said earlier, your distortion *is* the means through which you can resolve a deeper issue. When you meet your discomfort with a real sense of compassion and conscious engagement, those old wounds can start to heal and the psychological structures can begin to unify. While an out-in modality may provide some temporary relief, eventually the band-aid wears thin and your wound becomes re-exposed. So my issue isn't so much with the out-in modality as it is with the proclamation that deep healing has taken place. Band-aid modalities can be very useful and valid to some individuals at specific times in their inner development and their life circumstances. Yet I feel it's harmful to mislead individuals into believing that a band-aid is the deepest healing. Anyone can intellectually learn an out-in paradigm and therefore be qualified to teach it to others. However, if you want to guide people who seek a unifying experience that deeply heals and awakens from the inside out, you can't use a roadmap of labels, theories, or techniques to help you feel in control.

Frozen infant experiences are very hard to articulate because they make no rational sense to an adult. These experiences have to be physically felt. Only then can the nervous system and structures of the personality organically correct themselves. Only then can the missed stages of childhood development be completed while simultaneously integrating on all levels of your being. Understanding this inner dynamic intellectually isn't enough to bring about a self-correction, which is why talk therapy alone can't address it.

Adults with undeveloped reactive infant bodymind configurations may constantly need validation from others, since they haven't moved through the stages of development that allow them to trust their own instincts or feel their own moment-to-moment experience from beginning to end. However, if they have a fearful reaction to their experience of needing validation and support, they may shut down to their inner vulnerability, steadfastly doing everything on their own as an adaptation so they don't feel reactive to what they're genuinely experiencing. Essentially, they're looping around and around in an ongoing state of fear. They're functioning from a type of rigidity they perceive as independence. But this kind of control brings no ease to their inner dynamic. Instead, they're terrified of dropping the ball at any moment, believing they won't survive the experience. An alternative to this mode of functioning is to seek constant companionship as a way to regain the signal they need. Either way, they're seeking a signal that lets them rest comfortably into themselves.

If they feel rejected, they'll create more adaptations to keep themselves from feeling the intensity of their experience. This can come in the form of seeking pleasure in food, sex, romance, shopping, alcohol, drugs etc. In my work, I don't view this as an "addiction." I see it as an adaptation that allows them to keep functioning. The adaptations help them protect themselves from collapsing into a confusing and overwhelming state of fear or terror. That fear most likely expresses itself as a fragmentation or polarization that feels all-encompassing and never-ending. The adaptation is in place to help them remain sane—because experiencing the alternative in its original infant configuration could feel like insanity.

Inner Exploration Basics for Infant Dynamics and Early Infant Trauma

Undeveloped aspects of self that have been frozen and compartmentalized are stuck in time, so they remain caught in their experience. To move them on developmentally, you must compassionately validate and care for them as they are. However, you have to do this while you remain in contact with present-time reality. In other words, you don't want to re-traumatize yourself or the infantile aspect within you by collapsing into that reality completely. You need to be co-consciousness of both realities, exactly as they are.

When a mapping holds a tremendous charge, any trigger can elicit feelings of non-existence, death, insanity, or expansion, as if there were no physical boundaries. These feelings can terrify most people because they have no context for the experience and no way to restore continuity of their physical, mental, and emotional sense of self. The commonly used labels such as addiction, mental/emotional disorders, attachment disorder, panic attacks, chronic fear, PTSD, hyper-stimulation, codependence, depression, and out-of-body experiences might all be labels for reactions of the reactive infant bodymind. All can be rooted in the relationship to the infant bodymind. Individuals suffering from a reactive infant bodymind experience can become body-distant, meaning their relationship to their physical body is usually not very conscious. Of course, not everyone experiences the full impact described here; there are degrees to this type of distortion.

These somatic experiences, as well as the associations they carry, can feel very overwhelming and all-encompassing. There is always the danger of collapsing within the infant dynamic, creating an internal loop of reactivity where the threat of re-identifying with the childhood reactions becomes very real. *It takes tremendous self-awareness and proper support to consciously work with this dynamic.*

Typically, individuals dealing with early infant trauma have, to some degree, stopped having a conscious relationship with their physical bodies. So potentially, returning to this world of physical sensations can be overly intense or it can potentially provide a more direct means to connect with their distortions and eventually integrate the inner life from which they've separated. Doing this carefully, as I have suggested, creates the potential for the stuck experience to end its endless, ongoing, unchanging existence and finally have a beginning, a middle, and an end.

You need a lot of practice to consciously open and move into and through your full moment-to-moment experience. This includes feeling your contemporary body, while simultaneously feeling that part of you that's reactive to feeling your body. It isn't without challenges. Coming face to face with your inner imbalances can cause you to overanalyze or go rigid. If you overanalyze your reactivity, you can distort the natural flow between thinking and feeling, while "spacing out"—cutting yourself off from your physical body. Going rigid, on the other hand, lets you appear grounded, but internally, you become so rigid in your thinking and interactions with others that it limits your ability to not only consider other perspectives, but also remain conscious of the subtleties and *feel* what you experience on deeper levels.

When confronted, people who go rigid fear collapsing into the vulnerable reactions they hold within themselves. That fear leads them to avoid direct engagement. Their adaptive behavior might be forceful, dismissive, aloof, distant, cold, or arrogant. Of course, they don't see themselves as forceful, dismissive, aloof, distant, cold, or arrogant. The charge around this dynamic is much too great for them to consciously engage without help from an experienced facilitator. Having a good, experienced facilitator resources them differently so they can consciously feel into and through their distorted experiences while working to integrate their undeveloped aspects, personality, and nervous system. Also, it's impossible for them to continue re-formulating the same personas while they're going through the destabilization process that occurs as deep and natural healing takes place.

This highly charged, well-defended physiological dynamic represents another reason why it's important to include all the levels of your being (including the physical body) in your exploration. If you want to increase your potential for deep healing and integration, you can't skip steps or leave out any part of yourself. I've only shared a couple of examples of this inner dynamic, but there are many others. Even though I've only given you a brief overview of this concept, it's enough to provide a context for those of you struggling to have consistency and continuity within your experience of yourself. The next section provides an even broader perspective in which to do your exploration.

Chronic Hyper-Stimulation or Overstimulation

In graduate school, I studied Winnicott's Object Relations Theory, which describes how infants' relationship with their caregiver shapes their perception of themselves. According to Winnicott's theory, infants do not need perfect mothering, just "good enough mothering" so they can comfortably rest into themselves through each developmental phase. Children who have a secure foundation through an appropriately responsive and available caregiver are more likely to develop an autonomous sense of self. Children who don't receive good enough mothering will likely show signs of stunted developmental growth to varying degrees.

Good enough mothering, however, is not always easy to provide, since all humans are vulnerable to primal urges and karmic mappings. Early life experience can be brutal for primates. Infants cannot fend for themselves. They are completely dependent on someone outside themselves for survival. Children experience this on many levels. Consider their dilemma for a moment. Infants can't do the simplest things we take for granted, such as turning our heads. When infants want to move their heads from one side to the other, their caregiver has to do it for them. Worse, they can't even effectively communicate their desire.

This unfulfilled need becomes an inner distress. If this distress isn't alleviated, infants discharge the energy by crying, for example, until their caregiver picks them up. That act—when the caregivers pick up the infants and talk softly to them—takes the charge off and stops them from stewing in their own inner intensity. Physical touch can often release the stimulation or charge that children feel within their physical and mental/emotional experience.

In the initial developmental stages, infants don't even feel separate from their caregivers; they experience themselves however their caregivers experience themselves. If caregivers can't stay appropriately connected with their infants emotionally and physically, for example, the infants feel discomfort. One way this can happen is when children cry chronically but the caregivers don't pick them up—or if the caregivers do pick them up, but are "checked out"—then the children have to learn to adapt within their own limited resources.

If caretakers don't respond to infants by using soothing facial expressions, emotional connection, or touch, those infants may feel great distress. This distress can happen on every level of the children's being. The conclusions the children come to within their limited cognitive abilities get mapped onto their nervous system *and* their physiology. The infant implements a "survival strategy" whereby they become externally focused and internally unfeeling. They save themselves by trying to save the parent. Since infants experience themselves in a very black-or-white paradigm, they feel those inner experiences very directly and intensely. So when infants don't receive good enough mothering, they can hold their adaptations in a highly charged and polarized inner experience. Typically, children separate themselves (or at least their conscious awareness) from the experience as a way to survive the constant overstimulation that's held in a life-or-death polarity. And so, you can see that the imprinting is established very early.

If the original stress isn't addressed, it continues mapping throughout all the child's developmental stages. So from one incident (or the same incident repeated a number of times), children can develop many highly charged mini-polarizations. As adults, however, they can't intellectually understand these inner experiences since they make no sense in a mature context. While they grow into adults in the chronological sense, their personality structures and nervous system still carry this old mapping. Therefore, a traumatized six-year-old isn't necessarily emotionally or cognitively six years old because he's lost the continuity of his naturally evolving, developing sense of self that would have allowed him to be developmentally, emotionally, and chronologically six years old.

Because parents can't be there all the time for their children, every person carries from childhood some level of stress held within the bodymind. Hence the saying: "It takes a village to raise a child." The intensity of the charge depends on a couple of factors: the frequency and duration of the caregivers' neglect or intrusion *and* the degree to which the infant felt discomfort. At the same time, since the resolution dwells within the soul, the charge has a strong connection to the child's core belief or story that he carried into this life, which in turn impacts how he reacts, as well as the degree to which the stress stays locked within his system. Paradox is inherent in life; therefore, the infants' karmic beliefs create and influence the type of experience he'll have within himself. So the child's beliefs and his/her relationship with the caregiver go hand-in-hand.

Love Addiction and Its Relationship to Infant Dynamics

The label "love addiction" describes what can happen when infants in chronic distress polarize their energy as a way to survive the intensity of early trauma. Since infants can't yet rest into themselves for comfort, they seek a connection with their caregiver as a way to feel comfortable at different stages of development. Infants await a signal from the caregivers that allows them to rest calmly into themselves. The caregiver may do this in many ways—with eye contact, physical touch, sound, and/or through a shared feeling.

Infants do anything they can to maintain this connection so they can relax. Losing that connection feels intolerable; the distress creates such an intense charge that adrenaline pumps through their little bodies as though their very survival were at stake. This creates a distinct imprinting that remains in the system as a distortion even as the children age. This distortion colors the way they experience themselves—

not only in relation to their inner sensate world, but also in their emotional relationship to themselves. In essence, it becomes challenging for them to know what they feel inside themselves since their inner terrain is so highly charged. Since emotions are an overly intense physical experience, they're forced to intellectualize their emotions instead of physically feeling them. In the long run, this way of functioning creates problems, given the lack of inner resources that children have in early development. But at the same time, this inner configuration also gives them the ability to relieve the constant assault from their own constant charge.

If this happened to you, you likely had to compartmentalize yourself as a way to remain comfortable while you developed chronologically. Over time, you lost your direct connection to these intolerable, highly charged experiences. You walled them off from your consciousness. Yet the imprinting stays intact even though you remain unconscious of it. This imprinting is what you experience within the physical, mental, emotional, and spiritual levels of yourself.

Your conscious or unconscious experience of that imprinting can bring on feelings of tremendous shame. You can't fully suppress the need for the caregiver's comforting signal, even if you use sex, romance, food, alcohol, drugs, over-working, spiritual seeking, or any other way to try to diffuse this intense charge. You might feel ashamed since you can sense that something isn't right within you. Deep down, you likely believe you should feel more adult or autonomous, yet the desire to relieve that deep early signal remains very strong.

So when psychotherapists use the term "love addiction," they're referring to individuals who desperately look outside themselves for the same signal they sought from their caregiver as an infant or young child. Adult "love addicts" keep looking for that signal because they're stuck in this inner dynamic that's being held and expressed within the body-mind. The experience never got a chance to complete itself because it's been walled off. *The adult behavior is a reaction to the stress of a long-ago moment.*

From the perspective of this work, your intellect by itself can't address this experience. You will need to address it on all levels of your being and in an organic way. A piecemeal or outside-in approach won't result in deep healing and integration. For healing to take place, you have to work consciously, layer upon layer. This allows the strong charge to diminish a little at a time while also allowing your body-mind to integrate. As you move through the stages of dependency and are able to remain engaged with each layer, you'll be delivered into a more autonomous and self-referred experience of self. The key here is to recognize that "love" is not what you're trying to get. You're looking for an external signal that lets you rest into yourself comfortably. This inner dynamic most likely won't be easy for you to heal. You have to feel and care for the inner aspects of self, expressed through your strong inner reactions, that most likely feel infantile or young-minded, while simultaneously acknowledging and existing in an adult body. Also, you won't see much conventional support for individuals perceived as co-dependent or love-addicted, because the label and/or the behavior is perceived as the problem to be overcome or tossed away.

This is another example of why I feel labels aren't genuinely helpful. The term "love addict" doesn't accurately describe the complex inner mechanics of the experience; therefore, it does little to empower individuals. Working from this blueprint doesn't allow a facilitator to meet a client at the unique place where this inner dynamic expresses itself. That's precisely why I don't use labels in my vocabulary. These labels poorly describe the very real and intense inner experiences that uniquely express how our bodymind is currently formed and functioning. The dynamic provides information for us, pointing where to bring our compassion and validation for our inner experience through a felt sense of awareness. Consistent, compassionate mothering, along with conscious care for ourselves, exactly as we are, is what is called for to successfully heal this inner dynamic.

From Trauma Recovery to Self-Awareness and Integration

The only way for you to conceive of yourself as an entity is through separation or division. But true spirituality is, in essence, a state of "no self." In the Absolute Realm, how can you have a true "sense of self" if everything is unified into pure consciousness? This is a direct realization of the spiritual path. Simultaneously, in a relative sense, you experience yourself as an individual being. If you intend to embrace both levels of being fully, you must integrate your experiences within your physical and psychological expressions.

If you experienced any level of trauma from your external environment or from internal reactions to your currently held beliefs (or both), you'll most likely come up against the myriad ways in which you implemented adaptations to keep you functioning comfortably. From the perspective of this work, you may need to cultivate a healthy psycho-physiological sense of self before you can live a fully manifest, spiritually awake existence. It's so easy to dismiss your current distortions as "just your personality," an attitude that does little to motivate you to mature developmentally. Even individuals who've awakened enough from their perceived separation that they won't easily fall back into their individual identified infant patterns still need to consciously integrate their fuller experience on all levels to fully embody their human and spiritual expression.

If you've experienced trauma, you'll have the additional challenge of feeling experiences that may be disorienting or overwhelming as you consciously engage self. Although you may integrate more slowly than someone who's not dealing with trauma or abuse issues, you can still absolutely accomplish it if you work wisely. In fact, you might feel even more motivated to clear up your distortions than someone who doesn't feel the same type of intense charge, since you can't afford to get complacent if you truly want to heal. Compared to someone who isn't dealing with early life abuse and trauma, your consequences are dire.

Anyone can get caught in ego-identification at any time on the journey of awakening. I've known individuals who didn't experience much early life trauma, but are unconsciously caught by their own lack of ego development, while simultaneously functioning from higher states of consciousness. Anyone can get caught at any phase of development. No one is immune to it. It's important to remember that everyone did something—created some adaptations—to survive the mental, emotional, and physiological intensity of early childhood development and the human condition.

The Pitfalls and Setbacks of Awakening
on the Spiritual Path

As we evolve, we all endure pitfalls and setbacks. For example, some of us may seek a *preconceived notion of enlightenment*, hoping a transcending meditation or spiritual practice and/or a technique can provide a shortcut so we don't have to feel our uncomfortable experiences. However, it doesn't work that way. While we move along the spiritual path, our ego can be shocked when it discovers it can't avoid what it had hoped to avoid. As we organically become aware of the adaptations we've used to keep uncomfortable experiences suppressed, our conditioned mind tells us to keep functioning from the adaptation, and that can feel confusing. The voice of fear can be very persuasive, and many of us may go unconscious again in order to preserve a false self. It's typically a time when we disown our own intense reactions and consequently project them onto our facilitator or teacher.

This happens to everyone at some point as they evolve, but if you're aware of the dynamic, you have a greater ability to wake up and move all the way through it. It can be a tricky pitfall to navigate past. Do your best to not skip steps in your inner exploration. You really have to feel your way through this inner dynamic and question everything from multiple perspectives. Sincerity and complete honesty about how you function and what you truly value are windows for exploration as you slowly transition from "going unconscious" to "waking up within the highly charged identities" you unconsciously function from. In this phase of awakening, you have the greatest potential to wake up and directly experience the paradoxical nature of life and existence.

I know many individuals who'd like to evolve at a quicker pace, yet they admit that fully being with what is, feels intolerable. *Using the physical body as a resource to diminish the intensity of your experience enables a spiritual movement away from identity and toward Self-realization, even amidst tremendous intensity.* Integration is the key to this path. Use your pathology as information to point to where you go unconscious, as opposed to behavior patterns to be overcome.

If you've experienced trauma in your past, you'll need to proceed slowly, use the tools wisely, and respect the intensity of your experiences. Past trauma can feel very real when you're going through this process, which is why it takes tremendous self-awareness to wake up within the expression of a distortion. Take your time and go at a natural pace that lets you integrate successfully. Don't force anything. It takes time and experience to become adept at knowing when you can open to an experience, so it can release and transmute instead of letting it re-traumatize a reactive aspect that's caught within you.

To allow earlier experiences to complete and move out of your system a little at a time, you have to be with them *as they are, while simultaneously feeling the here-and-now.* You won't be able to sweep them under the rug because they'll keep coming up until you meet their conditions. Therefore, you'll want to learn and directly experience what they're doing for you. Don't underestimate healthy psychological development. *The human journey—along with its many stages of development—is in place for a reason.*

Some individuals Self-realize without much early-life trauma. Others Self-realize through a lot of pain and suffering. There is no right way. There is no *one* way. *Your* way is unique to you.

Another pitfall of the spiritual path is the ego's need to be seen or to experience itself as "special." It can seem like a natural phase of awakening to take on a persona of an enlightened or awakened being. This phase of awakening can be awkward because you may notice your need to be special—to be seen as more awake than everyone else—and you may try unsuccessfully to annihilate that need. If you aren't even conscious of it, others may reflect it back to you, by being either captivated by your persona or annoyed by it. If you've moved through a series of awakenings, you've most likely come up against this dynamic. It can be a tricky experience to consciously engage, especially because it can come and go. The key is to be sincere and completely honest with yourself about your inner motivations while exercising self-compassion.

As I became more conscious of it, I gave this aspect of ego the name "Miss Smarty Pants." I observed the way Miss Smarty Pants affected my behavior when I was around others. I'd vacillate between feeling righteously indignant about how much more awake I thought I was to feeling mortified by these thoughts and behaviors. I couldn't get rid of Miss Smarty Pants no matter how hard I tried. Eventually, I accepted it as a natural phase, which allowed me to be much more easy with it. My ability to be honest and take full responsibility was essential to my continued development.

Whichever direction your path leads you, the goal is to cultivate a seamlessly integrated physiology, one that includes the individual human expression along with the spiritual expression. The only place to start this work is where you find yourself right now. Remember, you're not trying to change anything, least of all yourself. You are eternal and divine, even if you've temporarily forgotten it—nothing and no one can change that.

The answers to everything lie within you. The answers aren't in a guru or a lover or a book, including this one. The answers are within *you*. Learning to "feel" and "be" with what is, however, is a prerequisite. As you do this work, you'll see for yourself how fruitless a preconceived notion of health can be. That's because as you consciously evolve, you end up surrendering all control, living what's real and authentic, and naturally moving with the flow of life. It's in your direct experience that your autonomy awaits you.

CHAPTER 8

Conscious Whole Being Integration: A Practicum

The most common question I hear from clients is: "How and where do I begin this process?" My normal answer sounds so simple: "Begin with what you're experiencing in your life and then move inward with your exploration." What you feel and how you react shed light on your beliefs and conditionings, but you most likely won't develop much self-awareness unless you can diminish the intensity of your experiences and slow yourself down enough to remain conscious of what you're really feeling. Your self-awareness increases as you track your moment-by-moment experience, which includes your reaction to it.

In this chapter, I've provided a couple examples of very basic integrative sessions. Since this is a foundational book, I'm not giving extensive examples—learning to work with the bodymind while tracking your energy flow is a very intricate and individually unique process. It takes considerable practice and self-awareness to consciously work on all levels of your being. These examples are meant to give you a basic understanding of how to do this work consciously and safely. At the same time, these examples may not necessarily reflect the right entryway into *your* conditioning.

Lesson One

Here's an example of my Conscious Whole Being Integration work in action. The following dialogue comes from a private session with a male client I'll call Sasha. A 42-year-old doctor, Sasha's been doing personal process work for most of his adult life. He started doing formal meditation and hatha yoga about ten years ago. While he's very sincere about his inner exploration, he came to work with me to consciously experience his whole being and accommodate his full experience exactly as it is.

Deborah: "What would you like to work with today, Sasha?"

Sasha: "I'm feeling very angry today."

Deborah: "I can see that. Want to tell me about it?"

Sasha: "Something happened at work, and now I'm afraid I'll lose my job because of it. I'm incredibly pissed off!"

Deborah: "Would it be OK if I help you to slow down a little bit?"

Sasha: "Sure."

Deborah: "Great. Sit forward in your chair, put your feet flat on the ground, and press them into the floor slightly. This engages your legs and slows down your rising energy, which will ultimately help you stop looping in your brain. We'll get back to your experience of anger in a minute, if that's all right."

Sasha: "OK."

Deborah: "Place both hands on the top of your head with your fingers relaxed and elbows forward. Gently move your hands, one hand forward and one hand back, as you advance forward and down your face. Now lightly stroke the skin down your throat. Be aware of your breathing. Feel all the sensations that you created."

Sasha: "I can feel them."

Deborah: "Good. Now rub your left shoulder with your right hand. Rub in a clockwise motion, then, begin moving down the arm rubbing back and forth across the arm until you arrive at your elbow. Make a circle around your elbow. After a moment, continue rubbing your arm back and forth until you reach the ends of your fingers. Now repeat this process on your other shoulder."

Sasha: "OK."

Deborah: "Great. Now arch your eyebrows up and down a couple of times while consciously feeling how your scalp moves. Move your jaw from side to side a couple times. Pause for a moment. Feel the sensations in your body as your energy flows. Again, notice if you're breathing comfortably. Are you with me?"

Sasha: "Yes."

Deborah: "Now place your hands on your hips and feel the sensation that creates. Move your hands down about an inch at a time until you get to your knees. Cup your knees and move your hands in a circular motion. Pause for a moment, then lift your left foot and lay it on your right thigh while you continue going down the leg. Rub the top and bottom of your foot slowly, feeling and moving with your natural rhythm."

Sasha: "It's not easy for me to feel my natural rhythm. But I just felt myself sync up with it."

Deborah: "Good. Notice if you're holding your breath or if you're breathing normally."

Sasha: "I was holding my breath. I'm glad you reminded me."

Deborah: "Now repeat the same thing on your right leg. Move with your natural rhythm. Feel each sensation. That's good. Now pause again."

Sasha: "OK."

Deborah: "Notice again if you're breathing comfortably or holding your breath. Feel all the sensations you created. If you feel someplace on your body that needs more support, feel free to touch or rub or even cover that area. Also, if you feel called to move your body in a certain way, please do so. Let it come naturally."

Sasha breathed evenly for a few moments. He seemed less agitated.

Deborah: "How are you doing?"

Sasha: "I feel a little frightened, and my solar plexus feels wide open."

Deborah: "Let's have you cover your solar plexus with the pillow on the chair as you feel your experience. Allow your experience to be as it is, while you observe and physically feel your sensations. Don't force anything."

Sasha hugged a pillow to his belly, rocking slightly forward and back, for several more minutes. Then he tilted his head and opened his eyes.

Sasha: "I'm also feeling some pressure on top of my head, toward the right side."

Deborah: "All right, bring your awareness there. Place one hand directly on that area and pull the hair up at the root for a couple of seconds. Let yourself feel the sensation that creates. Can you feel it?"

Sasha: "Yes, I can."

Deborah: "By bringing your awareness to your scalp, you'll help the energy that's stuck there move in whatever way it can. Your brain's becoming overstimulated from the backlog of rising energy. It can feel uncomfortable with all that energy looping around in your head. Don't try to direct the energy; let it move organically wherever it wants to. I hope this gives you some context for your inner experience. Does that make sense?"

Sasha: "Yes."

Deborah: "Now, starting at the top of your forehead on the right side, lightly rub your fingertips in small circles swiftly moving downward until you reach your eyebrow. Remember your feet; don't completely lose your awareness of them. Then, with an open palm moving in a circular motion, work all the way down the front of your face to your chin. Move your jaw side to side a couple of times. Now pause and feel what sensations you set in motion. Notice if you're breathing comfortably. Then reach up to the top of your head and slowly move your scalp backward and forward again."

Sasha yawned and his eyes watered.

Deborah: "What's your experience now?"

Sasha: "I feel much calmer, but I still feel angry."

Deborah: "OK. Let's see if we can work directly with this experience. Who or what within you is feeling angry?"

Sasha: "I am. I feel angry with my wife, my job, and myself."

Deborah: "Sasha, I've learned from years of doing this work that anger is usually about disempowerment. Does that resonate? Are you aware of some aspect of self within you that feels disempowered?"

Sasha: "I don't know. I never know what I feel. I always experience a type of oblivion going on inside myself. I especially notice it when I sit in the silent being meditation you taught me. I wish I were different. I try to force myself to be more present, but it never works, and I always end up feeling more like a failure than ever before. I don't know what to do. I gulp down energy drinks and caffeine throughout the day so I don't have to feel so depressed."

Deborah: "So would you say that you're experiencing a feeling of oblivion right now?"

Sasha: "Yes, but I don't know how to change it."

Deborah: "You don't need to change it. Your experience of oblivion is there to keep you from directly feeling something within you, possibly an experience that felt too intense for you when you were a child. You first have to recognize that this intensity is a feeling; it isn't you."

Sasha: "What do you mean?"

Deborah: "I mean it isn't the true you. It'll take time and considerable practice for this to become your direct experience. For now, it's enough to understand it intellectually. See, you think this is a self-esteem issue: 'If only I were better or different than I am, then I'd feel better about myself.' Let's look at it from a different perspective. Instead of seeing this as pathology—instead of asking yourself: 'What's wrong with me?'—let's explore it from the perspective of what it's doing for you."

Sasha: "What is it doing for me?"

Deborah: "Your body wisdom created a way for you to survive an experience that was way too intense to feel when you were a young child. So you blocked it off and kept it sealed inside you. This created an oblivion that helped part of you keep functioning and grow up without feeling the ongoing intensity of that experience. You use the coffee and energy drinks to match the inner intensity you currently feel inside. If you don't speed yourself up artificially, then you get caught up in your reactions to the overstimulation you constantly endure within your system. The good news is that it worked. Here you are in my office, alive and functioning."

Sasha: "I might be alive, but I don't feel . . . whole."

Deborah: "That's because the experience you had is frozen in time. It can't ever fully develop or complete itself; it can't ever change. All it can do is experience the same thing over and over. All feelings have a beginning, a middle, and an end when you feel them all the way through to completion. But here's the really important part in all this: you don't actually know it's a feeling. You experience it as an intense inner charge—so intense in fact that you've lost yourself to it and identified with it. Since you've walled it off, you aren't even conscious it's there. You feel your disconnection on some level—you can sense that—and you don't feel quite right within yourself. Additionally, because you've stopped physically feeling this experience in order to function more comfortably, all you can do is shunt back and forth within your polarized reactions."

Sasha: "Hmm. That seems right. No wonder I have to be on the go all the time. When I'm working, sometimes I notice that my heart's racing and I feel agitated, so I have to keep busy to distract myself."

Deborah: "When you have a thought and become reactive, you go unconscious and begin looping, thinking something's wrong with you. You tell yourself: 'If only I had better self-esteem. If only I could figure it out. Then I'd feel better. Then I'd have a different experience of myself.' So you've been dealing with this inner dynamic by disengaging from your physical experience and getting caught in your circular thought patterns and believing them. Because you're unconsciously caught in that inner dynamic and you're reactive to your current experience—while believing you are your thoughts and experiences—you try to change yourself from the outside in, hoping that it will make you think and feel differently about yourself on the inside. But as long as you try to be someplace other than where you currently are, you won't have the deep inner connection you're longing for. You have to be with what's happening, internally and externally, exactly as it is. You have to consciously feel and explore the experience of oblivion: get to know what it physically feels like and witness how you function from within it in your everyday life."

Sasha: "How do I do that?"

Deborah: "Well, first you have to be honest with yourself about what you're experiencing in the moment, exactly as it is. This sounds simple, but it can be very challenging. You want to notice how and when you go unconscious. Not to change it, but to develop a conscious relationship with how you currently function. For instance, where are you clenching in your body? Look at the way you're hunched over. Your eyelids are heavy too. There's a physical quality to the feeling of oblivion. See if you can feel that quality in your body. It's subtle, so pay attention."

Sasha: "Wow, I do feel it. It feels like . . . a kind of aloofness."

Deborah: "See if you can feel it as a physical sensation in your body. In what part of the body do you feel a relationship to this aloofness?"

Sasha: "I feel it in my heart and my abdomen."

Deborah: "What does it feel like?"

Sasha: "I feel some tightness in both areas . . . and a little nausea in my stomach."

Deborah: "Notice the relationship your heart and abdomen have to the feeling of oblivion. Don't force anything. There's no wrong answer here. It's just an exploration."

Sasha: "OK."

Deborah: "Feel what the oblivion is doing for you. As you bring your awareness there, ask if your heart or your abdomen would like to communicate anything to you. If not, just notice what the experience shifts into. It could move to another area of your body. Feel the sensations as they move through you. Observe it and feel it as it tells its story. Remember not to force it to shift in any way. Just allow it to tell its story in whatever way is honest.

Sasha: "Wow, Deborah, it's amazing. I just remembered an experience I had when I was a child. My parents were arguing. I thought my father was going to hurt my mother. I felt really scared. I can still feel it in my heart and my gut, like it's still there. It feels so real, almost like it's happening again. But I can't articulate the feeling. It's beyond any words I could use."

Deborah: "Sasha, listen to me. That's your perception of what happened when you were young. Do you understand what I mean by that?"

Sasha: "No. Are you saying it's all in my imagination?"

Deborah: "No, I'm not saying that at all. What you just expressed is what it felt like to you at that time. What actually happened in the room between your parents back then may have been different. Having said that, it's a fact that you felt the way you did. Both things are true. Different people can have different perceptions of the same incident. Your inner experience is just as valid as anyone's. There's not just one reality.'"

Sasha: "I think I understand. I wondered why the experiences I remember from my childhood are so different for me than for my parents. I always felt angry about that."

Deborah: "Good awareness on your part. Now you have another perspective to explore your experiences from. In order to cultivate a healthy relationship with this process, though, it's important to consider this past experience as a story. It holds validity for the aspect inside you that's caught in that experience, but it's not in any way, shape, or form an indicator of who and what you truly are. Over the course of this integrative process, you'll wake up to many stories functioning within you that you unconsciously reinforce. You'll learn to observe the story and even consciously interact with it in moments, while simultaneously physically feeling your relationship to the story. Along the way, you'll awaken to the direct experience that you are not the story."

Sasha: "Wow! I get it. Intellectually, at least. But I'm afraid that I'll forget it after the session ends."

Deborah: "That's all right. Having an intellectual understanding is just the beginning. As you're able to work with your current experience exactly as it is, you'll cultivate a physiology that will help you directly experience co-awareness. I say 'co-awareness' because you'll become aware of two things: one, your reactions that are caught up in past experiences and reinforced by your identifying with them; and two, your current ongoing experience of yourself in the here-and-now. You'll feel both inside yourself as your direct experience. Remember though: you can't force that level of awareness. It has to come naturally as you consciously move through the layers of your conditioning. There are levels of awakening and mastery, so when you've sufficiently mastered one level or phase, you'll organically enter the next. I'm meeting you exactly where you are right now, so you can accommodate what you feel and learn what you need to learn. Over time, as you feel more comfortable with whatever you experience within yourself, you'll effortlessly move with the natural flow of life. You won't resist your experience, even if it doesn't feel good. The physical embodiment and seamless integration you cultivate through this process will give you the ability to accommodate what is. All right?"

Lesson Two

The next example is from a private session with a 54-year-old woman I'll call Sophie. Sophie is an actress and a writer. She's been in therapy since she was 23. The following dialogue is from our first session together.

Sophie: "Hi, Deborah. It's nice to meet you!"

Deborah: "It's very nice to meet you as well."

Sophie: "I'm feeling very nervous, so I apologize."

Deborah: "Sophie, it's all right that you're feeling nervous. What brought you in today?"

Sophie: "I've been in therapy for so long, yet I feel like an open wound. For the most part, nothing has changed, and I've literally tried everything. Now I'm feeling all this panic and anxiety, and my health is deteriorating. I've had chronic illness for the past ten years. I go in and out of bouts with exhaustion. I've seen lots of doctors, but they can never find anything. I'm feeling depressed and over-whelmed by life. I've gained weight recently too. I tried every diet, even exercising with a private trainer, but nothing seems to work. I've been seeing a therapist who does cognitive behavioral work and art therapy, and together, we came up with some affirmations I can use."

Deborah: "What's your experience been since doing the affirmations?"

Sophie: "At first, I was very hopeful because it made so much sense. After all my years of therapy, I figured I needed to reprogram my thoughts and change my behaviors so I wouldn't keep experiencing the same sadness about my childhood. I feel so bad about my life and about myself. I have all these tools, and yet I still can't get it together. So I thought maybe doing the affirmations and changing my behavior would finally allow me to feel happy about myself again. I don't resonate with organized religion, but I've been practicing shamanism for the past couple of years. I feel more connected to the spirit world now. I channel a guide every morning, and she gives me the infor-mation I need to help me in my spiritual quest. I'm very fortunate to be able to go into the spirit world so easily."

Deborah: "So why did you come to see me?"

Sophie: "I want to feel my connection to all of life. I heard that you work with the whole being, so I felt it might be a good direction for me to go now. I feel like I'm sitting on a time bomb, but I don't know what to do about it. I experienced something within myself when I was a kid, and it terrified and confused me. Now I'm scared that I'll re-experience it. I get terrible panic attacks from it. Every therapist I've seen tells me I won't re-experience it since I'm so much healthier now than I was back then, but something inside keeps telling me they're wrong."

Deborah: "Sophie, I want you to try something. Close your eyes and feel into both your legs for me. Do you get a sense of both legs? Can you feel a subtle difference between them?"

Sophie: "I can't feel them much at all. They feel weak, like they're dangling from my pelvis. I feel like I can't keep my attention there. I go straight up into my head."

She began to weep.

Sophie: "I feel like I'm wearing a football helmet. I'm very anxious right now. I feel as though I'm going to leave my body. It's very disorienting. My brain feels very slow-moving, yet somehow I feel very speedy at the same time. What does it mean?"

Deborah: "OK, Sophie, open your eyes and look around the room. Notice what you see. You can get up and walk around a little bit if you like. Feel your feet as they touch the carpet. Would you do me a favor and smell a rose in that vase for me?"

Sophie got up and walked to the vase. She sniffed at the rose.

Sophie: "I wish I understood what was going on with me. And why are you having me feel into my body? I've never done this in therapy before. I'm used to just talking. Can you tell me what's wrong with me?"

Deborah: "Well, I can give you my assessment of how I think you're functioning, which is very different from telling you what's wrong with you. I understand that you feel uncomfortable with what you experience. You're used to therapists and physicians labeling you based on what they consider normal or healthy. You've been trying to fit their description of what you should look like when healthy, but by doing that, you've been avoiding what you genuinely feel. In turn, this creates a type of split within your bodymind. I can certainly understand your motivation. There isn't much support or acceptance out there in the relative world for being honest about what we genuinely experience."

Sophie: "What do you mean?"

Deborah: "Typically, when a therapist throws a label at us, it feels disheartening to our inner selves searching for reconnection. As soon as something makes us look less than perfect or not completely together, we go into solution mode. We're always looking for ways to distract ourselves from how we really feel. We chronically search outside ourselves for answers, as opposed to seeking an inward connection. You've probably been doing this most of your life. I sense the way you do it is to disconnect from your body and your physical experiences so you won't feel your own internal discomfort. This allows you to intellectually discuss concepts and theories about your feelings and emotions in therapy. That kind of treatment has its place, but it hasn't allowed you to physically or spiritually integrate your emotions. You need to include the physical body in your personal exploration to achieve this. That's why the focus of my work is about being with the individual human expression along with the spiritual expression. This work supports you as you move deep inside and consciously integrate all the levels of your being."

Sophie: "I was curious about that."

Deborah: "In order for your relationship with yourself to become authentically healthier, you have to learn to be with your inner experience as it is without trying to force it to change. This isn't about pleasing your therapist or even looking good to yourself or others for that matter. It's about coming into a fuller expression of yourself and being completely honest about the myriad ways in which you experience yourself. This allows you to begin to wake up and deeply heal the inner conflicts you carry from the inside out. Right now, you're in avoidance, so the best you can do is follow a therapeutic or spiritual technique to 'try' to feel an inner connection to yourself. Without that guidance, you're left vulnerable to your own distortions. So your only option is to emulate what someone else thinks you should look like when healthy because your internal experience is too intense for you to withstand on your own."

Sophie: "Well, that makes a certain amount of sense, but I think I've been getting something out of my years of therapy. I'm in a somewhat different place now."

Deborah: "I agree that you've been able to connect the dots

back to your childhood experiences, but you haven't integrated them with the other levels of your being. You aren't able to accommodate your experience as you are in the moment. Remember our little exercise? Your ability to consciously experience your physical body is challenged at present. If you essentially live in your head, you don't have to 'feel,' which you believe you can't handle. So you disassociate. This type of physical and energetic configuration keeps your physical body weak because it doesn't get the energy it needs. The channeling and shamanic journeying reinforce a pattern of going 'outside' for your connection to your Self. This in turn creates further weaknesses in your body."

Sophie: "But then how do I establish a spiritual connection if I don't do what I've been doing?"

Deborah: "You'll begin to feel a deeper connection to your essential self as you move through the layers of what you honestly experience in the moment. You're skipping this step. You're trying to be someplace you're not yet. If you really want to naturally integrate and feel connected to yourself, if you really want to follow your own natural inner rhythms, then going outside yourself for answers or creating a distorted relationship with the astral realm through channeling won't get you there. That's a shortcut to what you currently think spirituality is."

Sophie: "I just don't know how I can be with an experience that makes me feel so bad about myself . . . not to mention feeling really anxious."

Deborah: "You're already there. You're just kidding yourself by thinking you can artificially create a different experience to be an expression of your true nature. It will just be an expression of distortion, not true integration. Yes, the distortion is an adaptation that's helpful to some degree, but it has its limitations. Learning to feel your experience as it is and learning more about its relationship to your childhood means learning to feel, and for that you need to include your physical body. You live in your head as a way to function—you might even say as a way to survive. But surviving is not the same thing as living a conscious and fully engaged life. Every day, you avoid feeling that initial inner charge. At this moment, you'd find it impossible to go right in, locate that inner charge, and really feel it. Fortunately, this is a process that builds on itself. Integration happens gradually over time. It's not all or nothing. You've done a lot of work in the past and I applaud you for that, but you haven't integrated it with all the levels of your being to the point that it becomes your direct experience."

Sophie: "OK, I think I understand what you're saying. At least as much as I can right now."

Deborah: "Take some time to reflect on what transpired here today and decide for yourself how you'd like to proceed. It was wonderful to meet you."

Sophie: "Likewise. I'll be in touch."

Sophie worked with me for many years and did indeed become more consciously embodied and integrated. She no longer channels or does shamanic journeying as a way to feel connected with the subtleties of her true nature. She now lives a much more grounded and consciously integrated existence within herself.

She learned that she didn't consciously and physically feel many of the inner experiences she had walled off from herself. As she felt supported and validated in her inner explorations, she was able to move through the stages, learning to feel again. She felt more and more comfortable with her experience of herself in the moment as well. As a result, her self-judgment softened tremendously.

Sophie's relationship to her past childhood experiences also shifted more and more over time as she was capable of accommodating what she felt moment-to-moment with more clarity. She learned that the weight she was carrying gave her some much-needed protection from inner experiences that felt too intense. In essence, she learned that the weight helped her handle the internal charge. As she made that transition consciously, she moved into a more integrated experience of herself, whereby the weight naturally dropped away a little at a time. As she moved with the natural flow of life, consciously feeling her experiences, her weight reflected the degree to which she could comfortably accommodate her experience exactly as it was. In general, her relationship to herself became much healthier, and she remains in a very conscious and authentic relationship with herself and with life.

CHAPTER 9

Different Modalities and You

As you move through the various stages and phases of deep healing and awakening, your physiology goes through periods of imbalance as it rewires itself to come back into its natural rhythm. It's just what happens. Therefore, incorporating other healing modalities may at times be beneficial. As you move through the layers of conditioning, notice whether different parts of your physiology call out for support. Learning to "feel and choose wisely" is important to your process. One modality might encourage balance at a specific stage in your process. At a different stage, another modality may be just the thing to help you gain clarity about how you function. It all depends on what you need at the time.

As you learn to move with your natural inner rhythms, you'll gain a better feel for which modality can support your physiology. Each modality has a strength you may need at some point to assist your developing self-awareness. You have to work with your whole being to assist the natural unfolding of your consciousness. You don't know now what you'll need later.

Remember: integration happens degrees at a time. With each layer you encounter, use the various tools at your disposal to support your whole being. Sometimes, a good deep-tissue massage or a cranial sacral session can foster the most progress in your self-normalization. At other times, *pancha karma* detoxification might increase your awareness as your physiology naturally lets go of deep holdings and accumulated toxins.

As your physiology shifts, regular acupuncture sessions may address your energetic flow patterns and help your blocks and holdings self-correct, but look for a practitioner who understands that the goal is to open your channels only to the degree that you can comfortably accommodate more flow. Too much too soon is not helpful, and for some it can even be harmful. Additionally, sometimes acupuncture can help keep your energy grounded while you engage your current inner dynamics and clear them out of your system. Yet at other times while engaging your inner dynamic, it can feel too disorienting and overwhelming to increase flow through your system.

Consider whether herbal or homeopathic medicine can give your bodymind the appropriate and gentle support it needs. As you move deeply inside, fear states organically present themselves, which can tax your kidneys and adrenals. Herbal formulas that are right for your physiology can help tremendously as you move through the various stages of your inner development.

Most importantly, realize that your relationship with each modality is more important than the modality itself. If you find yourself just trying to "fix it," use this awareness as information about how you currently function and move inward to explore your reactivity.

You often won't know what modality will produce the most support, but if you can "feel" your way through the experience of *not* knowing, you'll begin to sense what direction to choose. Take it a step at a time and adjust accordingly. As you develop a clearer understanding of your relationship to everything, you'll be better able to choose wisely regardless of the level you're working on.

When deep healing and whole being integration is your goal, it can be advantageous to have access to a whole team of practitioners to support your integration. Since the healing process is subtle, however, every member on your team ideally should employ a natural and holistic approach. If just one practitioner on your team uses an out-in perspective, it can throw off your momentum and hinder your integration. Paradoxically, sometimes life presents us with certain challenges for which it makes sense in that moment to use a modality that isn't completely natural, but might help you in the short term. Just do your best to pick practitioners who are comfortable including the whole picture, as well as different perspectives. If one practitioner tries to force a correction on you or thinks his specific modality is the *only* way, I'd encourage you to look elsewhere. Follow your intuition.

You can find healers and teachers anywhere; it doesn't take much to hang a shingle. Finding one who functions from a truly integrated physiology and awareness, however, isn't so easy. It takes tremendous self-awareness to become a *genuine* healer or teacher. It's important that you choose to work with a person who consciously functions from what is. Effective healers must remain honest, open, and consciously engaged with the full expression of *themselves* in order to track and feel the nuances within *your* physiology that are striving to come back into balance. Any healer worth her salt will walk the talk.

Remember that your physiology is unique. Some individuals experience chronic physical imbalances while others float in and out of balance. Whatever your experience, it's yours. Do your best not to compare your physical, mental, or emotional health to others. Don't assume one way is better because it works for someone else.

Living Consciously

As you cultivate more self-awareness and integration, you'll feel your connection to the whole of life to a much greater degree. Instead of living on autopilot as a way to diminish the intensity you experience in relation to the inner conflict of your many selves, those selves slowly unify, allowing you to accommodate a fuller relationship with yourself. You'll begin to notice the incongruence between your direct experience on the inside and how you live your life on the outside. Life constantly tests you to see if you can live from the lessons you've just learned. This stage allows you to complete the integration. Therefore, it's important to pay attention to the relationship between your direct inner knowing and your external actions.

Establishing a healthy lifestyle and living environment is vital to successful healing. *The most important component of healthy living is to live consciously.* Observe your life. Notice how you spend your time. Ask yourself if you feel connected to and truly value what you're doing. Move in deeper and explore your relationship to what you value. Most people have no real connection to what they do, at least not on a feeling level, which reinforces the constant disconnection from their natural flow. It can be very enlightening if you begin to pay attention.

For instance, notice what television programs you watch and what music you listen to. Notice what you *feel* before, during and afterward. Once you have more information about what you do, how it makes you feel, and what it's doing for you, you can start making wiser choices. Notice your relationship to a particular show you watch or certain music you listen to. Observe whether you have any judgment about what you discover. Can you use it as information? This inner exploration engages you on a deeper level, allowing you to carry out this activity consciously and become aware of what the show or type of music is doing for you, as well as what you're reinforcing.

The key to this process is becoming conscious of your inner experience and naturally harmonizing it with your outer world. This allows you to make your own choices instead of adhering to a set of rules that has no real connection to you. For example, if you regularly exercise to the point of exhaustion, you likely won't get the results you want. When you exercise, feel the connection to your physical body. If you zone out about what you're feeling, whether your goal is long-term health or short-term weight loss, then you're continuing the same pattern of disconnection. Instead, feel into your body, whether at work, at play, or at rest. You don't have to be militant about it. Just innocently notice what you feel. *Stay interactive with yourself.* Find the type of exercise that intuitively speaks to you. Allow it to change as your needs change. Listen to and feel your body.

Additionally, it's important to get the proper amount of

sleep for your physiology. Ayurvedic medicine, an Eastern Indian practice that predates Chinese medicine, states that being asleep before 10 p.m. and rising by 6 a.m. aligns you with the cycles of nature and allows your bodymind to feel healthier and more relaxed. Some people, however, need more sleep than others to feel rejuvenated. Find what works best for you.

The type of fuel that we feed our bodies is equally as important as the exercise and lifestyle that we choose. Therefore, educate yourself on diet and lifestyle habits to find what fits you. If you're interested in "eating consciously," consider eating pure organic food that helps your imbalances self-correct. I personally feel it's important to know where your food comes from. I support organic farmers, not factory farms. I want to support those who take pride in their crops and care about the humane living conditions of the animals they raise. If you eat animal protein, make sure your animal products are free from antibiotics, steroids, and growth hormones. It's best if the animals are pasture-raised and grass-fed instead of being kept in pens or cages. Make sure their feed is non-GMO, certified organic, and vegetarian. Whether you realize it or not, you ingest the energy of whatever you eat, so eat as consciously as you live. We so often zone out when eating, leaving us in an unconscious relationship to all of life. As a friend once said, "If you're going to eat animal protein, you should at least once hunt and kill the animal yourself." Then allow yourself to have a direct connection to what you feel during the entire act. In our culture, we've lost any real empathy for the sacrifice animals have been forced to make in order for us to live our lives in such an unconscious manner.

Experienced, licensed acupuncture physicians or Ayurvedic practitioners can assess where you're out of balance in the moment by examining your tongue and pulse. Then they'll use the proper protocol—whether it's acupuncture, *moxibustion, marma point* technique, lifestyle changes, *pancha karma* cleansing, *shirodara,* herbs, or foods—to bring your physiology back into balance and clear out accumulated *ama* or toxins.

There isn't one diet that fits everyone. There can't be. There are too many different physiologies, too many different cultural backgrounds, and too many different food allergies. Besides, the food that brings about better health for you now will likely change over time. Feel into what your internal experience and your external body tell you.

Another tip I've learned along the way is to drink pure water—filtered or spring—with a pH as close to 7.5 as possible. Store it in glass instead of plastic. Water hydrates us and flushes out impurities. I prefer water that's warm or at room temperature, since cold beverages dampen the digestive fire. Poor digestion leads to many physical imbalances.

If you pay attention to what you eat and drink, you'll notice what feels right for you. Allow it to change as needed. Your body may need different types of foods and flavors at different periods in your life; therefore, it's advantageous to look at food as medicine that helps you either remain balanced or come back into balance. Also, it's important to learn what foods help you to remain in balance in relation to the time of day and season you're in. For example, during the summer months when it's hot outside, it's best to eat foods that are cooling in nature to counteract the external heat that raises your body temperature along with the outside temperature.

If you're interested in broadening the scope of your awareness to include your living environment, learn more about how to keep your environment as free of pesticides and chemicals as possible. You can find so many natural alternatives for every area of your life—from building materials, paints, sealers, and home cleaning products to pesticides for the garden and lawn. Protect the planet, your pets, and yourself from unnecessary toxins that can potentially cause harm over time.

If you want to align with nature to the highest degree possible, consider building a Vastu-friendly home from natural materials. Vastu, or *vastuvidya,* is the ancient Eastern Indian science of architecture that aligns with the laws of nature. In my living environment, I pay special attention to the energy flow inside my home. I'm conscious of whether the *qi* is moving at a harmonious pace throughout my home. I'm also aware of clutter. Every item carries a particular vibration, so I'm mindful of the vibrations with which I fill my home. While many books on Vastu living exist, they sometimes contradict each other. Do your research and make your choices based on what you feel through your own direct experience.

I'm also mindful of the amount of electromagnetic pollution throughout my home environment. Inform yourself about the dangers of EMFs with regard to WiFi, cell phones, cordless phones, iPod chargers, computers, and televisions. Take sensible precautions when using these devices. It's advantageous to your overall health, however, if you can limit your exposure.

Lastly, I want to mention the Vedic Science of Astrology, also known as Jyotish. This ancient knowledge is a science that can track your karma. If used in a grounded manner, it can help you view your life path from multiple perspectives. I use it as a tool to wisely guide me through the many stages and phases of my life and spiritual development. I don't use it as a crutch or to replace my direct inner knowing. Like other facilitators, a highly skilled Vedic Astrologer isn't easy to find. Do your research. Look for someone who is grounded and has a good reputation. My advice is to begin a professional relationship only with a Vedic Astrologer with whom you feel a sense of harmony and resonance. Unless you can understand and assimilate the interpretations of your readings, they won't be helpful to you.

Vedic Astrologers may recommend remedial measures—such as saying mantras, having *yagyas* performed, or wearing gemstones—to help you consciously navigate the patterns of your karma. Remember, though, that astrologers are human; they can make mistakes in their readings. It's your responsibility to use the readings as information. Again, less is more when it comes to remedial measures. Ultimately, you must feel within yourself and sense what feels right for you. I'd never encourage you to override your own inner knowing, but I *would* recommend investigating the source of the inner knowing to be sure it isn't coming from a distortion such as fear. Only when you're conscious can you be clear about how to best proceed . . . in *any* endeavor.

Medical Modalities

The knowledge I teach is about consciously and naturally embodying a full expression of your being—the divine as well as the human. I thought it appropriate to list practices that I personally found helpful on my journey. This section isn't meant to be a guide; it is meant as ideas that might help you choose your own path.

I've found, for myself at least, that classical homeopathy can do wonders to support the unfolding of certain mental/emotional trauma that created a physical imbalance. Homeopathy compliments the integrative work I teach. The practitioner you choose, however, can make all the difference in how effective it is. Find someone with a good reputation who works from a true, holistic place. Do your best to make an informed decision.

Allopathic or modern Western medicine has its place if used wisely, too. It can help keep you functioning in your everyday life. Although I generally use it as a last resort, it's a "quick fix" that's sometimes necessary.

Medication for a mental or emotional imbalance does not help bring about a natural self-correction. In other words, it does nothing to truly heal you. It can, however, dampen an intense internal charge enough to give you the time to do your self-exploration work more comfortably. Possible side effects, however, can be the price you pay for this type of medicine.

As with holistic medicine, it's important to find an allopathic practitioner who doesn't force your physiology to move in a certain direction or look a certain way—unless it's a life-or-death situation. You function the way you do for very good reasons, so use your diagnosis as information and notice where you become internally reactive. Find a practitioner who supports your natural unfolding, not one who puts you in a box so you just *look* healthy. *Healing is both an art and a science; it's not a race to the pharmacy.* It takes time to cultivate wisdom. So find someone who's comfortable fielding questions about the process and about your expectations. You have every right to know how a practitioner will work with you. See Chapter 10 for more advice about choosing the best facilitator for you.

Some of my personal favorite medical modalities—when used properly—are Chinese herbal medicine and acupuncture, Ayurvedic medicine and *pancha karma* cleansing, classical homeopathy and flower remedies, cranial sacral therapy (as long as the practitioner doesn't try to force a shift), and bodywork such as acupressure, reflexology, and massage. I've benefited from Swedish, deep tissue, Thai, and lymphatic massages at different times. I believe hands-on healing energy work can have value too, but be careful of practitioners who have a preconceived notion of what your energetic flow or energy centers should look like when healthy. In every modality, you can find practitioners who'll try to force a shift in you, either physically, emotionally, psychologically, or even spiritually. If this happens to *you,* it's in your best interest to move on.

I also feel a deep appreciation for organic movement in the form of dance and hatha yoga as healing modalities, if you can follow your own inner impulse and corresponding flow. I personally don't take classes where I have to follow a teacher. Mimicking a teacher, in my opinion, doesn't allow your physiology to organically unravel its blocks and holdings. When you aren't inwardly focused moment-to-moment, the bodymind doesn't integrate seamlessly, which I feel was the whole point behind ancient yoga. I much prefer to follow my internal experience and inner impulse. Additionally, I also like gentle *qi kung* and *tai chi* as healing modalities.

If this advice resonates with you, find a class that allows you to remain engaged with *your* inner rhythms. In these classes, students feel their way to the next movement, pose, or stretch. This type of environment fosters a more natural inner flow, not a rigid set of exercises. If you pay attention, your body will show you where you need to bring your awareness so the blocks in your flow can self-correct.

You can also include *pranayama,* a breathing technique, or other forms of gentle breath work, to help bring more balance to your bodymind. But practice discernment. While proper breathing aids the physiology, I don't recommend using breathing techniques exclusively to open blocks and holdings. Nor do I recommend using breath to force the movement of kundalini to produce certain states of being.

Trying to blast open a block before you have the ability to accommodate the new energetic flow comfortably won't bring about seamless integration. Instead, the distortion just reinvents itself again and again until you can remain engaged with what is, exactly as it is. Remember, blocks and holdings are in place to buy you time until you can remain conscious of what you couldn't before. Again, the immediate goal isn't to get rid of blocks and holdings, but to explore your relationship to them, thereby creating the potential for self-awareness and self-correction to take place. There are no shortcuts, as I've said throughout this book.

Spiritual Modalities and Meditation

During my journey, I've found that meditation and sound vibration are powerful practices for evolving my consciousness. These practices have helped me enormously by allowing the stress and holdings in my physiology to release and self-correct, which helps increase self-awareness. In truth, however, *every* experience has the potential to raise your awareness and increase your evolution—as long as you notice where you go unconscious and then do the necessary inner exploration to make the transition into conscious awareness of what is.

The meditation practices I found genuinely useful through the years have been ones that felt natural and effortless. The meditation practice I offer to individuals is called *silent being*. It naturally came to me after years of learning various types of meditation from other teachers and noticing what did and didn't feel helpful. *Silent being* doesn't ask you to force thoughts out of your head or try to artificially create specific states of awareness.

In *silent being* meditation, you don't have to sit in a rigid posture, unable to organically move when you feel called to. You meditate only when you feel truly called. Meditation opens us to truth. If you're already feeling more open than you can comfortably accommodate, the last thing you will *feel* called to do is to meditate and open yourself up any further. *Trust that inner feeling.* Just sit comfortably in silence and let everything be as it is. You'll sink effortlessly into the depths of your being rather than trying to dive, push, or struggle. It's almost as if you let meditation happen rather than actively pursuing it. Like genuine healing, you just have to set up the right conditions for meditation, and nature does the rest.

You decide both the length of time to sit in silence and the frequency with which you feel called to do it. It might be daily or weekly. It might be for six minutes or for sixty. Do it whenever it feels natural to you. Find your own rhythm and listen when you're being led to sit again. You have to discover what works for you.

The goal in meditation is to bring about the natural unfolding of your true nature. Again, it should feel natural and effortless. Here are some other tips for doing the *silent being* meditation. Every meditation practice needs to be slightly adjusted as you evolve, so keep in mind that this version of the meditation might not be the exact right fit for you in this moment.

Allow yourself to sit in whatever way feels comfortable. If sitting doesn't feel natural, then lie down. Do what feels natural to you. When you're comfortable, just notice what you notice. If it feels authentic, close your eyes. Notice what you feel, hear, smell, and taste. Don't force anything or try to change anything. Just let it be as it is. Remain silent unless it feels authentic, organic, and natural to make a sound. As you sit or lie there, innocently witness your thoughts moving through you. Don't force them out; just allow them to be what they are. Don't follow your thoughts, however—let them go as you witness what's present while you remain in deep silence. Feel your way.

Silent being allows you to go much deeper within. It allows you to listen at a deep level. Effortlessly feel what is in all its subtleties. For instance, if your awareness takes you to a holding in the solar plexus, allow yourself to just be with it. Don't try to figure it out or make it unravel. Just sit with it as you would sit with a close friend, letting it be what it is. Feel yourself as awareness itself. If you become reactive to what you see or feel, then observe what's reactive inside you while also feeling the place within you that remains non-reactive. Effortlessly experience yourself on the different levels of your being.

In doing this meditation, you learn to organically and effortlessly flow with your inner movement. Innocently notice what remains as your thoughts and reactions move through you. Feel the deep silence within. Allow yourself to be with the mystery of what you don't know or understand, as well as the fear of what is known. Again, just notice what you notice and let the flow of your inner experience be organic. If your body wants to naturally move, allow it to do so. For instance, you might feel your spine undulate or your shoulder move in circles. Let the body find its natural impulse.

Since you're already healed and whole deep within your being and since all knowledge dwells there, you can go deep within to inquire about the truth of your existence. Ask an exploratory question that really matters to you, and then be silent. Listen deeply without expecting an answer. Allow yourself to rest within. Let the answer come in whatever way is right for you. You may not get an answer or you may find that after you open your eyes that you feel inclined to write as a natural flow of subtle hearing moves through you. You may not get the answer you hoped for. You may even get an experience that feels uncomfortable. Nature isn't biased toward what feels good. *Truth is its natural expression.*

If it feels right, spend some time after each meditation reflecting on your experience. Discernment is an important tool during this exploration. Don't analyze your experience; just reflect on it, gathering more information about how you function. When you're ready, get up and move your body in whatever way feels natural to you, following your own natural impulse.

At times in your process, you may feel inclined toward more silence. Listen to that inner yearning. Like many of you, I've had periods in life when I've felt more social and periods when I've felt more inward. Both can last for days, weeks, months, or even years. I feel my way with it and adjust my life accordingly. This way of living feels authentic for me, but it might not be authentic for you. The point is that *everyone* has an authentic way of moving through life. Your goal is to find yours.

Find what you feel drawn to, but allow it to change over time. My only suggestion is that your meditation practice be effortless and natural. As you evolve over time, you'll naturally let go of the witness state, when instead of being aware of everything moving within you, you become the awareness. Remember—don't try to force or control any aspect of your being.

I've covered a lot of ground in this chapter, so let me just remind you that it's important for you to do your own research. I've only given a brief overview of each topic. In general, if a certain modality or path doesn't feel right, don't follow it. It really does need to speak to you. Before dumping it, however, do some inner exploration to make sure that your reservation isn't an expression of your distortions. Feeling the subtleties here can make all the difference. Discernment is a vital skill for concluding what feels right and makes the most sense. Also, be aware that your experience can change moment-to-moment. What doesn't feel right in this moment might feel right two days or even two hours later. Relax, feel deeply, and adjust accordingly.

CHAPTER 10

Finding Your Facilitator

A facilitator—whether man or woman, spiritual teacher, bodymind practitioner, healer, or psychotherapist—is a partner in your process of integration. Working with someone skilled and experienced in the integration process can make all the difference in the world. You might have one facilitator for years or even decades, or you might find that perfect person to help you through a specific stage or past a certain obstacle.

The decision to work with a facilitator to help your integration process is not one to take lightly. Choosing the right person to guide and support you is one of the most important choices you may ever make. A great facilitator is one of the biggest gifts you'll ever receive. A bad facilitator can be your biggest nightmare. Listen to your intuition, practice discernment, and choose wisely.

Searching with Discernment

Every experience in life has the potential to bring more self-awareness and integration if you can remain consciously engaged with your full inner experience. So don't drop your common sense at the door when you enter a facilitator's office. They are human and can make mistakes. Don't hand anyone the key to your health. Listen to what they say and then feel inside yourself to check it out. Ask yourself if it feels right, and then track where the source of the inner information came from before you make your choice.

Make sure your facilitator and you are both on the same page. If the facilitator becomes annoyed or inappropriate, then maybe you should look for someone else to work with. Empower yourself. Walk out if it doesn't feel right.

When working with your undeveloped aspects, you can feel particularly vulnerable. During these periods of your development, you aren't yet able to show up as a fully rational adult. It's vital, therefore, to have a facilitator with a solid reputation, but more than that, your guide during these trying times should be grounded, honest, and sincere.

If the person you're working with hasn't traveled down the vulnerable journey of exploring his own experience as it is, then he won't be able to support you properly. Since integration is a physiological process, your facilitator must have cultured an integrated physiology himself. This type of work isn't for the faint of heart, so find a practitioner who's conscious of the pitfalls and setbacks that can take place.

If your facilitator becomes unconsciously reactive during your session, he'll lack the ability to see you clearly. It's very important for all teachers or facilitators to remain present and track their own inner experiences so they can wake up any aspect that's caught in reaction. Not one person walking the planet today is completely beyond the capacity to go unconscious. I don't care how "awake" that person is.

Therefore, be cautious of teachers who feel they are beyond this inner dynamic.

A teacher or facilitator needs to see your patterns of conditioning clearly. I can tell you from personal experience that it can feel daunting to help guide someone to move into and through an experience if you haven't already done it yourself over and over. Your facilitator needs to have the confidence to work with you without a manual or step-by-step guide. He must meet you *where* you are, exactly *as* you are. Your facilitator has to feel his way throughout your process, knowing when to nudge a little and when to back off. The act of integration isn't easy, swift, or painless. Your facilitator has to be ready for almost anything.

It's also extremely important to pick a facilitator who supports you to think freely, someone who isn't looking to create a following. You don't want someone who will feed off of your dependence. Eventually, you'll naturally want to individuate from the facilitator, to continue your journey either alone or with a different person better suited for your next step. So find someone who supports that process in a healthy manner.

You might think it would be relatively easy to find someone to support you in this way, but it isn't. Facilitators are human, and they have personalities of their own. If they aren't continuing their own inner exploration—even while practicing their craft—they can lose perspective. If they've set up a situation in which you can't be honest with them about when you see that they are going unconscious, they might dig a deeper hole for themselves, often without even realizing it. Remember, you have the power to make informed choices; facilitators should work *with* you, for the process of healthy integration that *you* require. You must therefore be responsible for your own development.

The Student-Teacher Relationship

Spiritual teachers are sometimes the equivalent of spiritual rock stars: they can acquire a type of fame within their sphere of influence. They might become accustomed to student devotion. It can be a seductive situation for *anyone* to navigate, but it's especially tempting to a personality driven by an unhealthy or brittle ego interested in power.

I've seen this become a problem time and again. It seems to be inherent in organizations that have a single person in charge. Licensed therapists have a license and a reputation to protect. Spiritual teachers, on the other hand, don't have to adhere to a set of ethics or risk a reprimand by a licensing board. Of course, having a license does not make a person an ethical therapist. It all has to do with the individual, which means you have to rely on your discernment.

We've all heard of teachers using their power and authority to exploit their students. You can find many examples of this in American culture. Some teachers have had sexual relations with their students, which has caused emotional harm. Others have created cult-like followings where students forego their own common sense in order to become "enlightened" by the "master." Students resonate with their chosen teacher. On some level, they have something to learn, whether it's working in the positive or the negative. Regardless, this dynamic is rarely acknowledged openly.

In a student-teacher relationship, a karmic bond can develop on both sides of the equation. Teachers can also resonate with their devoted students. Without the students' karma, they wouldn't need the teachings, so the teacher can be unconsciously dependent on the students for their own distorted reasons. Both parties often have something to learn from each other.

How this relationship fits into the teacher's psychodynamic landscape is what matters most. The teacher's goal should be to support the students' gradual process of awakening, deep healing, and integration, since it's most important that the students have their own direct experience of the teachings. This allows the students to experience the phases and stages that are right for their development. If teachers don't explore their own reactions to individual students, the teachings might be unconsciously distorted relative to those students. The teacher's personal conflict resolution skills might become biased, if they aren't already limited and undeveloped. Needless to say, this situation can cause problems in a group dynamic.

The negative aspect of such a situation is that it can create an inner bind for some students, feeding a lack of development as well as a dependence on the teacher that causes them to consciously or unconsciously override their own inner knowing. Psychologically, the bond between student and teacher corresponds (or maps onto) that place where the affected students have been stuck in their childhood development, reinforcing their identities, beliefs, and conditionings instead of freeing them from those limiting factors.

There is a positive aspect to this scenario too, however. If students develop and mature enough to validate their experiences for themselves—even if the teacher denies it—they can create an opportunity for personal autonomy, further development, and individuation from the teacher.

Some of the best advice I received in my own process came from a Vedic Astrologer. "What makes a great teacher," he said, "is to be a great student. Always be a teacher *and* a student." Many teachers don't follow this simple but vital piece of wisdom. It's important, therefore, to recognize that all teachers are also having a human experience. They can be very well intentioned but just plain wrong in their behavior or their individual perspective. The student-teacher relationship should be one of ongoing mutual respect.

Both parties can distort the subtleties of the teachings, as well as their relationship to them, in any number of ways. Both parties must hold themselves personally accountable to maintain the written (or unwritten) contract regarding the social rules of their interactions. Both must practice discernment with regard to their interpersonal experiences.

Some lessons, at the wrong time or for the wrong student, can be unhealthy. Teachers should change their methods as necessary, depending on the students, situations, or any number of variables. Everyone on the planet is constantly evolving; it only makes sense that lesson plans should evolve as well.

Students need to remember that capable teachers are rare. If you're lost to your own inner conditioning and identities, you're vulnerable. Only a good teacher can help you find your way into and through those distortions. This is why discernment is so important. However, don't assume that working closely with a teacher will be comfortable. A teacher is there as a guide to help you awaken to your blind spots and "see things as they are," which may not be comfortable. Just like life, waking up isn't without its risks. If you're able to be very honest with yourself, you'll eventually learn an important lesson.

Keep doing your own inner exploration so you can

become clear about your inner motivations. Even though students want to be completely open and honest with the teacher for their own inner development, that does not give them license to be abusive or disrespectful to the teacher. A great teacher is a blessing, and if you resonate with one, consider it a rare gift.

In Conclusion

As a general rule, never do anything that doesn't feel right to you. Never abandon your own inner knowing. Many spiritual teachers and psychotherapists can be very charming, dynamic people, which makes it easy to follow them and forget your own common sense. Be wary. Let a facilitator continuously *earn* your trust.

You'll undoubtedly make mistakes; we all have. As soon as you feel that inner pinch screaming out to you, do your best to pay attention to it. It can be painful to feel your facilitator shut down on you when he's feeling triggered within himself, but that's part of the process of individuation. I've personally been involved on both sides of the situation, and it's a much sweeter transition when the facilitator happily supports your individuation and autonomy.

In summary, look for a facilitator who functions from integrity. Find one who is honest, compassionate, and comfortable with a challenging, questioning client/student (in other words: you). Work with someone who supports you in your experience as it is, keeps the work about *you*, has good physical and emotional boundaries, and can hold himself accountable for his behavior toward you, all while challenging how you act from and identify with your conditioning.

Also, I wouldn't suggest working with a facilitator/teacher who channels guides or uses past life personas to gain credibility or a following. Channeling can be harmful to the physiology—it isn't something a person who has cultivated integration in her physiology would practice.

I'd also recommend that you make sure the person you choose to work with speaks from his own direct experience. Don't work with someone who teaches from an outside source such as a book authored by someone else. Don't work with someone who has no direct experience of the teaching for himself. It takes time and commitment to be able to cultivate an integrated physiology, but only then can a facilitator speak from his own direct experience.

Furthermore, find someone who wants you to think for yourself. Beware the teacher or therapist who tells you what to do all the time. A teacher isn't meant to keep you from suffering. He's an experienced guide who supports you as you navigate the layers of your own karma, giving you the greatest potential to wake up to how you currently function. The pace at which you learn must always be honored and respected.

Finally, when speaking with a facilitator or teacher for the first time, don't shy away from asking about the level of inner work *he's* done on a personal level. You don't need to get invasive, but it's important to know whether this person can work from what's real and true for you without trying to fix it. Anyone who's done this type of work will genuinely support your personal empowerment. Ask if he works in a holistic manner. If he's comfortable with your interview, it's an excellent sign that he's a good candidate to help you on *your* journey.

So once again: *listen to your intuition, practice discern-*

ment, and choose wisely. Good luck on your personal journey toward Conscious Whole Being Integration.

A Final Note

My intention for writing this book was to give you a foundation from which to set out on your own inward journey. Because of all its inherent subtleties, however, this journey isn't something I (or anyone) can teach you. There are no steps to follow. It's something you need to experience directly. Any teaching that has any value points you back to yourself. Having the foundation that this book offers isn't meant to keep you from thinking for yourself. Quite the contrary. The tools and teachings I've shared are meant to help guide you as you move deeper inside yourself and consciously make your way through your experiences. If you try to adhere to these tools and teachings as a way to control the outcome of your process, then you aren't using them wisely.

Your relationship with the teachings in this book will make all the difference in your ability to integrate. Since there are equally valid, yet simultaneously contradictory realities, consider different perspectives at every phase along the way. What feels true for you now at this stage of your development could change as you evolve, so experience each layer honestly and authentically, proceeding at your own pace, while observing and questioning your relationship to everything. Most importantly, remember this: throughout this book, I've shared parts of my unique journey. It in no way defines what *your* unique journey should look like. While there may be similarities, each of us has a unique journey to experience. It's up to you to discover yours.

About the Author

Deborah Hall has pursued her quest for universal truth and wisdom with a single-minded focus and a certain fierce adherence to principles. Her studies of psychology, bodymind integration, energy healing, meditation, and other Eastern spiritual traditions and practices led her to spend nearly two decades moving deeply inward. She created a private retreat lifestyle for herself, spending much of her time in silent meditation and self-exploration while moving naturally through the many stages and phases of deep healing, awakening, and whole being integration.

In addition to her academic work, she has done in-depth study under the guidance of teachers in bodymind integration, Ancient Vedic knowledge and science, and spiritual enlightenment.

In her study of psychology, Deborah earned a Master's degree in Clinical Psychology from Antioch University in Los Angeles, where she gained a deep understanding in Object Relations Theory, Family Systems Theory, and Trauma Resolution. Deborah also holds a license as a Marriage and Family Therapist in the State of Florida and a Bachelor of

Science degree in Business Administration from Florida State University.

Through her personal in-depth studies, she developed the ability to perceive and track her own energetic configuration, engage her patterns of conditioning, and clear her energetic distortions. Through these processes, she established a deep, natural way of restoring a more harmonious energetic life-force flow. Her direct experience has given her the ability to guide others through this challenging journey.

It is her long, deep personal study—combined with her academic foundation and professional experience—that has given birth to and nurtured her own teachings: Conscious Whole Being Integration.

For more information please visit: DeborahHall.net and ConsciousWholeBeingIntegration.com.

Made in the USA
San Bernardino, CA
16 May 2017